To Mary Florence + friends.

Thank you for always praying for us & our family —

May God continue to richly bless you!

Albata & Gene

ALL THINGS NEW

2015 – 2016

ALL THINGS NEW

2015 – 2016

Wayne E. Fowler

2017

Acknowledgment

Except where otherwise indicated, all Scripture quotations in this book are taken from The New American Standard Bible ®, Copyright © 1960, 1962, 1963, 1968, 1971, 1972, 1973, 1975, 1977, 1995 by the Lockman Foundation. Used by permission.

First Printing: 2017

ISBN 978-1-365-76581-0

Wayne E. Fowler
287 Crawford Road
Blairsville, GA 30512

www.mountainchristian.net

Contents

Foreword

This book is a collection of articles I originally prepared for the North Georgia News, Blairsville, Georgia during 2015 – 2016, as indicated by the date of publication noted with each title. These are also posted at www.mountainchristian.net.

The newspaper column is for pastoral topics. My goal is to inform, educate, challenge, inspire, and motivate believers and non-believers via theology, current events, history, politics, philosophy, arts, and literature, a tall order for short articles! My limitation was column length, hence the brevity and occasional lack of thoroughness and continuity. I appreciate the grace and intuition of the reader. Some of the original articles are lightly edited herein for space and clarity.

I have included Scripture References and a topical Index for your use.

Thanks to my dear wife Laura who faithfully read each article and offered much-needed editorial comments.

And He who sits on the throne said, "Behold, I am making **all things new***." And He said, "Write, for these words are faithful and true" (Rev. 21:5).*

WEF

Finish Well

January 7, 2015

I'm not big on New Year's resolutions. I doubt I'm alone, especially by the time Valentine's Day arrives. It seems better to think about finishing something, not just trying hard to start something that should have been done a long time ago anyway. Surely you've heard a sage in your life say, "don't start something unless you can finish it."

I am a Georgia man, but Auburn educated. Early this football season I enjoyed the high ranking of so many teams from the SEC West, and all the chatter about how dominant our division was. Such power made it easy to explain away the intra-division losses. Commentators crowed about the possibility of two SEC West teams in the new playoff scheme. Problem is, we didn't finish well. Auburn didn't, for sure, unless you count a new defensive coordinator as the highlight of the season.

Finish well. That's not a goal, but a lifestyle, which applies to faith, too. I have observed in over a half century of life and decades as a pastor, there is a caricature of faith that turns away the unbeliever and discourages the believer, so neither finish well. G. K. Chesterton said, "Christianity has not been tried and found wanting; it has been found difficult and not tried." The past is a graveyard of good intentions slain by the belief that Christianity is just a strict and high moral code to keep.

The Apostle Paul said, "I have fought the good fight, I have finished the course, I have kept the faith" (2 Tim. 4:7).

Was it traveling the world, planting churches, shaking a snake off his hand, speaking to rulers? Was it keeping all of his New Year's resolutions that led to this conclusion? Doubt it. He finished well because he counted "all things to be loss in view of the surpassing value of knowing Christ Jesus my Lord" (Phil. 3:8).

This caricature of faith I mentioned omits the relationship. Authentic faith is about the person of Jesus, God the Son, the one who loves you. It embraces change wrought by God. Consider that "it is God who is at work in you, both to will and to work for his good pleasure" (Phil. 2:13). Faith in Jesus means a new life lived by a moral code written on the inside.

Seems that God would be more than willing to answer the prayer, "if you're really there, let me know you." Finish well by finding the surpassing value of knowing Christ. Come to think of it, that would be a good New Year's resolution!

"Behold, I stand at the door and knock." - Jesus (Rev. 3:20)

Enduring Faith

January 14, 2015

I first noticed his British accent. Later I learned that what he had to say was even more impressive than the way he said it. I was at a conference a few months ago, and sat down to enjoy breakfast with my fellow attendees. It was providential that I sat next to Rob Gifford, the China Editor for the Economist magazine.

He is certainly credentialed for the job: Harvard-educated, fluent in Mandarin, well-traveled as documented in his book China Road. Our conversation quickly turned from polite acquainting to my persistent questioning. He recently completed an article, "Cracks in the Atheist Edifice," and I was anxious to hear the details.

He spoke of a city, amazingly nick-named "China's Jerusalem" due to its population of Christians. Many churches there that do not meet in homes have had their buildings demolished recently. This sad destruction notwithstanding, the communists are gradually allowing more religious freedom in China. Some members of the ruling party are now Christians, and many believers are emerging from the shadows to active roles in the community. Many demographic experts agree that there are now more Christians than communist party members.

China has a long history of Christian missionary work. Robert Morrison translated the Bible to Mandarin by 1819. Coming later were Hudson Taylor, Lottie Moon, Eric Liddell, Bill Wallace, and Bertha Smith. Many missionaries to China, including some of these, were ignored, arrested, imprisoned, tortured, and murdered without seeing much fruit from their labor. If they could only witness the growing tribe of Christ-followers in China today!

They knew our God is not restrained by time. We tend to look for results now if we sacrifice or serve, but sometimes the check is cashed after we are gone. Endurance is a trait of the faithful, regardless of results seen in this life. We cannot faint from past failures nor rest on past successes.

Where does this endurance for faith and life come from? It comes as believers from Georgia and England share news of the faithful in China. It comes from an awareness of those who have gone before and who finished well. We are a community that spans time and geography, bound by our common heavenward gaze upon the One who authored our faith.

"Since we have so great a cloud of witnesses surrounding us, let us also lay aside every encumbrance and the sin which so easily entangles us, and let us run with endurance the race that is set before us, fixing our eyes on Jesus..." (Heb. 12:1-2).

It is a difficult world we live in, but we are not without hope. We know Who to trust, and how to have an enduring faith.

Missional Living

January 21, 2015

I have a friend who once patted his ample belly and pointed to his waist-line. "This ain't a belt. It's a leather fence around a chicken graveyard!" I share his taste for the most common species of bird in the world, so I welcome the news of Chick-Fil-A coming to our town.

But it's not just their recipe (other eateries have good chicken, too!) that's attractive. Their founder, Truett Cathy, adopted a corporate purpose statement that includes this: "To glorify God by being a faithful steward of all that is entrusted to us." The business environment he created attracts dedicated people who must not check their faith at the door of their workplace.

A Facebook meme reports that the manager of a Chick-Fil-A in Birmingham noticed a homeless man that came in to escape the cold. He found warmth from the manager who gave him his gloves and a free meal, inspiring the patrons who witnessed the kindness.

This simple act, not meant to be noticed or published, captures more about the latest churchy buzzword "missional" than many books that try to explain it. Missional is a new attempt to explain old ideas about faithful living.

Christians are a sent people. As Christ was sent to us, he sends his followers on mission to a world darkened by the absence of Truth. He said, "You are the light of the world. A city set on a hill cannot be hidden...Let your light shine before men in such a way that they may see your good works, and glorify your Father who is in heaven" (Mat. 5:14, 16).

Authentic faith roams freely and acts unexpectedly, not displayed behind stained glass, illuminated by chandeliers. It notices and addresses people, their hurts and needs. If the totality of religion is to attend a service or volunteer for an activity, is that a life that exists to glorify God with all that is entrusted to it? Is that a life that serves others in a way that makes them wonder 'why would you do this?'

Western culture is increasingly post-modern and post-Christian (i.e. everyone can have their own truth except Christians). Yet if Jesus gives us the grace to love our enemies and pray for those who persecute us, then a kind act, generous gift, encouraging word shouldn't be too hard to muster. It lights the world when a Jesus-affected life reflects the love of God to the human condition.

We say we want to be like Christ. Well, consider that his ministry was incarnational, (he touched people personally), and sacrificial (it cost him). Missional living can be no less, can it?

Trustworthy Source

January 28, 2015

As he approached the rim, he began to smell the smoke. The terrain and rocks under his feet were a color and texture foreign to his experience. Suddenly he was there, and his gaze fell deep into the crater toward the glow of fire in what the locals call, "The Mouth of Hell," the Masaya Volcano in Nicaragua. Wrestling with his sense of danger, it helped to recall inspecting the eerie confines of a witch doctor in Haiti and braving the murderous streets of Ciudad Juarez.

This could begin the fictional, fanciful tale of an unfulfilled adventurer. But it could be a true story with witnesses still alive that could authenticate the details.

A fabricated story widely published as true wouldn't take long to unravel. That's what happened in 2003 when Jason Blair lost his job with the New York Times over made-up stories. Perhaps worse, journalist Janet Cooke had to return a Pulitzer Prize for a story she fabricated. Late in 2014, the false Sabrina Erdely story in Rolling Stones magazine did great harm to the University of Virginia. In these cases people read the stories and knew they were not true, and made noise about it.

This idea forms one of the reasons you can believe the Bible. It is not a collection of philosophical musings or arbitrary morality. It is a narrative that contain specific details of places, times, and people while revealing truth about God and us. Wouldn't it make sense that if God were to reveal truth via the written word, He would include historical, verifiable details about real people so it would be plausible? Indeed, at the times the various books of the New Testament were written, the people in the stories were still alive! The books were copied and distributed far and wide, with no fear that someone in the story would show up and declare, "Hey, that didn't happen!"

Paul makes that point himself, writing about all the people who witnessed the resurrected Christ, "He appeared to more than five hundred brethren at one time, most of whom remain until now" (1 Cor. 15:6). He was using their experiences and living witness as proof of truth. Besides, why would Christians maintain a collective lie while enduring the withering persecution the early church faced?

The Bible is trustworthy. Sure, it has been misaligned, misused, and misunderstood. But its purpose remains to reveal that God invites you to trust the Jewish Messiah, sent to take away the sins of the world. That's good news!

By the way, I'd be glad to recount the tales of my travels to Nicaragua, Haiti, and Juarez to anyone willing to listen (and I have witnesses)!

Finding Freedom

February 4, 2015

In his recent book, <u>Why Suffering</u>, Ravi Zacharias recounts a conversation with an inmate in the infamous Angola Prison in Louisiana: "I asked him, 'How do you handle the prospect that you will never get out of here, and that this is where your life will now be spent?' He answered, 'You know sir, if you knew the kind of person I was before I came here, and what I have now become because of the freedom Jesus Christ has brought to my soul, I can only say that if this is what it took to bring me to my senses, I am happy to spend the rest of my life here.' Then he paused and said, 'Please pray for my parents. They think they are free, but they are in a prison of their own darkness without God.' That evening it was all I could do to fight back the tears as I watched this same man leading more than 700 prisoners in worship."

There is a man changed by freedom, though in prison for life! Christians believe that Christ sets us free, which implies that we are in bondage. It's usually offensive to suggest something's wrong to someone who didn't ask, but consider me a former prisoner trying to show others the way out.

Look, life is not supposed to be like this. Temporary love, broken trust, and subjective truth are too common. Children are at risk, addicts choose wrongly, and money is loved. The Ten Commandments are treated as just ten suggestions. Our churches can be showcases for saints instead of hospitals for sinners. We do what we don't want, and don't do what we do want. We have conflicting passions and goals. Such is the human condition – it is bondage, and it hurts.

What can you do? Attend meetings, join something, set new rules, cover bad by doing good. But all that just leads to more bondage. If you've tried it, you know what I mean.

The Hebrew prophet Isaiah foretold a Savior who would release captives and set free the oppressed. Jesus claimed to be the fulfillment of that message. He explained that if we continue in his word, we are his disciples. His disciples know the truth which sets us free. Free indeed, but from what? Free from the demands of the law by his gift of grace. Free from sin to live godly lives. Free from death to be eternally alive. Author T. W. Hunt says, "God's intention is that we be free from this world's mind-set. In doing that, God binds us to His mind-set, the mind of Christ."

God accepts and forgives according to your faith, not how well you perform. By faith, he transforms your mind, and your life reflects Christ. By God's grace, that is freedom!

A Love Story

February 11, 2015

I stepped from the evening cold into a room warmed by the stove in the corner, and by the welcome of a man who has pastored for over 50 years. I sought writing insights from Danny Parris, who has yielded this column space, at least for now. As we sat by his wall of well-used books, I listened to his heart for people as he shared his story.

I finally asked about the subject at hand, love and marriage. "Well, marriage is of God, instituted before the church," he started. I injected, "Tell me about you and Regina?"

"I asked God to give me someone to love, and to be loved by." Danny doubts the notion of "falling in love," but believes that God chose Regina for him. Perhaps evidence for that was their first outing together, a double date when he thought he was paired with the other girl! But it was Regina that sat next to him in the car, and the rest is history.

"Well, marriage is about leaving, cleaving, and weaving." What a wordsmith! Actually that comes from Scripture: "A man shall leave his father and his mother, and be joined to his wife; and they shall become one flesh" (Gen. 2:24). Stories from his life unpack that idea.

The young Parris family left parents, church, and Fannin County in a U-Haul and VW after church one Sunday night, moving to New Orleans. Leaving means starting a new life together, finding your own way.

"Everything we have done, we have done together." Cleaving is having Regina as his partner in life and ministry, so she is always close by. In a service, they usually sit together until sermon time. A friend dubbed their pew "the love seat!" Stepping into the pulpit, he will "look for God, then Regina" before he starts.

Sometimes hardship weaves lives into one. It was hard to hear of his nearly tragic crash in a '52 Ford with his expectant wife and son. But through it, God firmly called them into their life's work. "I can see the hand of God at work in difficulties, learning the lessons of life."   Good times and bad weave lives into one.

Please don't let this example of a long, loving marriage cause you regrets.   Danny has seen "so many people thrown on the scrapheap of life." No, this example of a faithful relationship gives hope that the love of God is real, and can reach into our world and even touch you.   The New Testament uses marriage to teach about Christ's love for his church. You are included in that great love. "For God so loved the world that he gave his only Son, that whoever believes in Him shall...have eternal life."

Pondering 55 years of marriage, Danny declares, "I love her far more today than when we first married."   Still weaving, I suppose. Happy Valentine's Day!

Racing For Change

February 18, 2015

At the National Prayer Breakfast this month, the keynote address was by NASCAR great, Darrell Waltrip. He told of two racecar drivers, and what made the difference between the two.

The first went at it all the wrong ways. People called him brash, ruthless, pushy, cocky, conceited, aloof, boastful, arrogant, and downright annoying. The fans hated him. The drivers despised him. Richard Petty once told him "I don't know how you keep a sponsor." His personal life was mess. He drank too much. He did everything to satisfy himself. That was his lifestyle.

The second was a driver popular with the fans, respected by his competitors.

Waltrip was both drivers. In his words, "In 1983, my horrible wreck knocked me 'conscious.' It was a wakeup call. If I died would I have gone to heaven or to hell? I thought I was a pretty good guy, but good guys can go to hell. I started attending church." In time, with his wife and the preacher, "I got down on my knees and prayed that the Lord would come into my life and forgive me of my sins and be my Lord and Savior."

"That changed everything. I felt like a new man! I knew I was different. When the Lord comes into your life you're going to be different. You have to be different. The Lord changed me for the better. I still had wrecks. I still had problems. But now I wasn't in it alone."

He was describing the life change that accompanies conversion to Christ. He discovered a basic Christian doctrine, that right living is not the way to right relationship with God; it's the other way around.

This is a theme in Romans 6: "As Christ was raised from the dead through the glory of the Father, so we too might walk in newness of life." "Our old self was crucified with Him…so that we would no longer be slaves to sin." "Consider yourselves to be dead to sin, but alive to God in Christ Jesus." "Sin shall not be master of you, for you are not under law but under grace."

If you concede that God has an ethical demand on your life, surely it is good news that you can truly know Him and be empowered to live rightly! By faith, you participate in the change. By faith you are in Christ, and in Christ you no longer have to yield to sin. People are not independent; either we are subject to sin or to God. God's grace is the only power which can break the mastery of sin.

I appreciate Mr. Waltrip's account of his life. Look for his humorous, heartfelt speech on YouTube. He may have had a 30-year career turning left, but he turned out right!

Science and Faith

February 25, 2015

At a recent international trade event in London, a BBC reporter asked Wisconsin Governor Scott Walker, "Are you comfortable with the idea of evolution...do you believe in it?" Walker "punted" the question as a thinly veiled attempt at ridicule. Perhaps he could have been more prepared.

Behind the question is the belief that science has settled the ultimate questions of life, so faith-informed answers are irrelevant. Science is the means to explain away the existence of a Creator. Some in the faith community are eager to accommodate, which renders its doctrines incoherent, and dismisses its texts as metaphor.

Science should not be so confident that its present "conclusions" on a subject will not change. After all, the scientific method requires hypotheses to be challenged by new data. In the early 20th century, the common scientific position was that the universe had no beginning. Philosopher Bertrand Russell defended this conclusion as sufficient to end any further debate about God's existence.

In the 1960's a new hypothesis gained support in the scientific community, but met resistance from the atheists. New data suggested that the universe began at a point in time. That in itself does not prove the existence of God, but it does realign a scientific conclusion to allow that possibility. Kings College Professor (and former atheist) Alister McGrath wrote, "This fundamental shift in the scientific consensus has changed the tone of the debate about God. It reminds us how science changes its mind about very important things."

In 1998, philosophers William Lane Craig and Anthony Flew re-debated the issue that Russell "settled" decades prior. In light of the Big Bang Theory (not the TV show!), Craig applied this logic: Whatever begins has a cause; the universe began to exist; therefore, the universe has a cause. Flew found it difficult to argue otherwise.

Not long after, Flew renounced atheism. He may not have embraced Christianity, but he at least admitted that science cannot answer ultimate questions. Regarding the origin of the universe, he wrote, "If you had an equation detailing the probability of something emerging from a vacuum, you would still have to ask why that equation applies." It seems quite unreasonable to think that the universe caused itself for no reason.

It is more reasonable to consider an outside cause, such as the Christian doctrine of creation, which speaks to the act and the reasons for it. "The heavens declare the glory of God; the skies proclaim the work of his hands" (Psa. 19:1). In Fatherly love, God created a world that makes Himself known to created people.

After the interview, Gov. Walker clarified saying, "Both science and my faith dictate my belief that we are created by God." Faith and good science can coexist as they point to the same truth.

Don't Worry

March 4, 2015

I have a doctor friend that once explained to me that the human body is not designed to handle worry and stress. He cited an assortment of diseases of the heart, stomach, and skin that can be the body's warning signs. Yet we worry.

I recently took an informal poll of friends at church and strangers in a store, and I found the usual laundry list of things that burden our minds. We worry about health, finances, and relationships in the past, present, or future. We worry about things near (driver's license) and far (global politics and economics).

The Bible has much to say about the world as we experience it, and worry is no exception. The Biblical word for worry is literally a "divided mind." Max Lucado writes, "Anxiety splits our energy between today's priorities and tomorrow's problems. Part of our mind is on the now; the rest is on the not yet, the result is half-minded living."

So to that end, I offer five ways to become "whole-minded." Jesus said it much better as recorded in Matthew 6, and I urge you to read it for yourself.

1. Understand what life is. It is more than human needs. Embrace difficulty as an opportunity to persevere and succeed. Our character and convictions are forged in the fires of trials, which make us who we are.

2. Realize your value. You are made in the image of God, and are an expression of his loving, creative touch.

Even if you don't think He exists, He loves and values you. Surely, then, you do not walk alone.

3. Stop controlling. Yeah, everybody knows a control freak, but this is not about them, but you! Worry does not add to your life or solve problems, but it certainly takes something out of you and makes things worse. Some things are simply beyond your means to control, so in the lyrics of the movie "Frozen," "Let it go"!

4. Live in today. Each day has enough cares of its own. There are too many things that can change by tomorrow whether you worried about it or not. Do what's in your means to do now.

5. Trust God. Worry and trust are awkward companions. Trust cannot demand that God be your fixer, but it does accept that He is near and personal. He may not move the mountain but will walk with you over it. Seeking God and pondering the treasures in his Word leave little room for worry.

Don't be that jokester that says, "Worrying must work for me! Most of the things I worry about never happen!" Stuff happens, but don't make yourself sick worrying about it.

Goodness!

"I'm good" has become quite the humorous way to buffer a "No!" When asked if we want something, the negative response is "I'm good." Such as, "Do you want a coffee?" "I'm good." Or, "Let's walk on the ice over that lake!" "I'm good."

The idea of goodness has worked its way into the conversation about the existence of God. Philosophers have posed the question, "Can we be good without God?" I would be out of my league to engage those thinkers, but some thoughts come to mind. Perhaps this will get you to thinking, too.

Notice the question doesn't demand belief in God. Sure, there are non-believers who do good things. The question is really about how we know what is good.

The secular answer is that our morals come from ourselves and whatever evolution has built into us, including survival of the fittest. As products of random chaos humans have no more intrinsic value than other species. So the value of a person and her morality are subjective. What or who she values is her choice.

The theist responds, how do you define good? When you acknowledge good and evil, that's a moral law. Skeptic philosopher Immanuel Kant said, "Two things awe me most, the starry sky above me and the moral law within me." If there's a moral law, there must be a moral lawgiver. Moral law is innate to the value of a person.

Where could that value and the moral law within us come from, if not God? Could molecules or chance do that? If there is good, there is God, so we cannot be good without Him to define it.

The God Christians know is loving and just. His moral commands are not arbitrary or random, but are an expression of His character. We are accountable, and our choices have eternal consequence. He values us enough to provide a Savior to balance the scales of justice, and enable us to live lives of moral consequence today.

William Lane Craig wrote, "If God does not exist, then it is plausible to think that there are no objective moral values, that we have no moral duties, and that there is no moral accountability for how we live and act. The horror of such a morally neutral world is obvious. If, on the other hand, we hold, as it seems rational to do, that objective moral values and duties do exist, then we have good grounds for believing in the existence of God."

The story goes that a wealthy young man approached Jesus with a question. Jesus answered, "There is only One who is good" (Mat. 19:17). Without God to define good, the question of good without God cannot even be asked! So, the next time someone answers you, "I'm good," perhaps the follow up question is, "How do you know that?"

Community

March 18, 2015

Dietrich Bonhoeffer was a Christian pastor and theologian during World War II. He led a clandestine seminary in Germany for the Confessing Church, in defiance of the Nazis. His experience living in close quarters with those pastors at Finkenwalde led to his book Life Together. Later, Bonhoeffer chose to join a plot to rid the world of Hitler. Tragically, he was captured and hanged by the Gestapo in April 1945, shortly before his concentration camp was liberated by the Allies.

He begins this book with, "How good and how pleasant it is for brothers to dwell together in unity" (Psa. 133:1). Then he develops his thesis that Christian community "is not an ideal which we must realize; it is rather a reality created by God in Christ in which we may participate."

Humans are created for community, which you might define as people with common interests networked by relationships. We experience that through associations, civic clubs, and charities. Our kids' schools, sports, and hobbies are other ways we connect. Maybe the "Cheers" sitcom was right. We just want to be "where everybody knows your name, and they're always glad you came."

Christian community is profound and unique because it is founded on Jesus Christ. Believers share the life of Christ, and so belong to one another. Together, we are the "body of Christ," an expression of Christ in the flesh. Frank Viola (Reimagining Church) challenges us "not only to proclaim the gospel, but to embody it by its communitarian life."

How does the church embody the life of Christ? Consider how many times the Bible uses "one another" in addressing the church. We are not only members of one another, but are to pray for, be devoted to, submit to, and be of the same mind with one another. Christians honor, accept, admonish, greet, and serve one another. Perhaps the most difficult is to "bear with" one another.

Bonhoeffer famously warns of loving the dream of community more than community itself. Life can be messy when lived in close quarters. The antidote is agape or sacrificial love within the church (1 Cor. 13). Show me a church that has loved its way through a crisis, and I'll show you authentic community. Living in community is a privilege that we too easily forego. Bonhoeffer urges us to be thankful for what it is, since complaints only "hinder God from letting our fellowship grow according to the measure and riches which are there for us all in Jesus Christ."

So now I ask you, Christian, who are you living your life with? You might be missing out on something.

The Sacrifice

March 25, 2015

After studying journalism and law (Yale), Lee Strobel became an award-winning journalist at the Chicago Tribune. His wife disrupted his secular life when she announced she had become a Christian. Though pleasantly surprised by the change in her character, he remained skeptical of Christian claims of history and truth. So he systematically interviewed experts in history, science, medicine, and psychology looking for answers. You can read about it in The Case for Christ.

We are in the midst of the season celebrating the central events of the Christian faith: the death, burial, and resurrection of Jesus. Despite the evidence, skeptics remain. Some question not only his death by crucifixion, but that Jesus even existed.

First-century historians Josephus, Tacitus, Pliny, and Thallus mention the Jesus story. From these sources, we find that: Jesus was a Jewish teacher that many believed performed miracles. Some believed he was the Messiah, but not the Jewish leaders. He was crucified until dead under Pontius Pilate, but his followers believed that he continued to live. His following spread into the Roman world in the first century as people worshipped him as God. All of this from non-Christian sources!

The Bible adds historical details to these accounts. The Jewish leaders killed him because he was a perceived threat to their authority. The Roman governor Pilate killed him, and washed his hands in front of the crowd to symbolically exonerate himself of innocent blood.   The angry mob killed him because they chose the known criminal Barabbas to be released and shouted at Jesus, "Crucify Him!"

So if a real Jesus lived and died, the next question is, "Why?" I was enjoying lunch with a fellow once, when he pronounced that he respected Jesus because "he died for what he believed in." I almost choked. To him, Jesus was just some revolutionary, an activist that got what was coming. Didn't his death mean much more than that?

A Hebrew prophet tells us, "The Lord was pleased to crush Him, putting Him to grief" (Isa. 53:10). Think of Jesus' tortured death, then read that He "for the joy set before Him, endured the cross" (Heb. 12:2). Yes, joy! People may have carried out the death sentence, but it was God's plan all along. Why? For us, for love. Before the foundation of the world, God knew we would fall into sin; in love He prepared a Sacrifice to bear our sin and offer forgiveness. His call is believe Him and accept what He has done for us. It's life-changing.

What became of Lee Strobel? He was convinced by the evidence, and believed that Jesus lived and died on his behalf. Might you also need to consider that you are the reason for the Sacrifice?

The Resurrection

April 1, 2015

This week, Christians are celebrating an event that fulfilled ancient prophecy, surprised early believers, and validated the claims of Jesus. His Resurrection is so central to the Christian faith, that skeptics know instinctively that if it is proved to be a hoax, then Christianity falls like a house of cards. In fact, Scripture offers that point almost like an invitation to investigate: "If Christ has not been raised, our preaching is vain, your faith also is vain" (1 Cor. 15:14).

As you might expect, it has been investigated. Christians have logical reasons to believe that Jesus came back to life after he died, even though believing the Bible is enough for most of us.

An early cover-up is recorded in Scripture. The people that won their capital punishment case against Jesus were so concerned about his claim to rise from the dead that they posted a guard to stop the theft of his body. These same guards later reported angels, earthquake, and an empty tomb, but received bribes to say Jesus' body was taken.

His foes could have proved the Resurrection a hoax by simply producing Jesus' body. They couldn't, so they propagated their own deception to blame on his followers. At least we know that friend and foe knew that the body was gone.

But is the empty tomb enough to believe the resurrection account? Consider the behavior of the disciples. Immediately after Jesus' death, they huddled behind locked doors fearful that they would meet his fate. Perhaps they just hoped to return to their former lives. What a defeated bunch!

Here is the illogic. Why would such a group concoct a cover-up and maintain it against the religious and political power-brokers that were determined to end Jesus and his following? Why not simply write down what he said as an inspiring teacher and avoid further controversy? Why declare in public venues and at their trials that Jesus was not just a good teacher, but arose from the dead and is the expected Messiah, the living God? They looked their accusers in the eye and said they would obey God rather than men. Would the eye-witness followers of Jesus have suffered and died for what they knew to be a lie?

Is the Resurrection just a metaphor, and did his followers invent the Christ of faith from the historical Jesus? It is far more logical that Jesus' followers were emboldened by something shocking, terrifying, and exciting. Only a bodily Resurrection after a gruesome crucifixion and death could have transformed them so.

If he did return from death, then Jesus is as He claimed, "The Way, the Truth, and the Life," and our faith is not in vain. In His Name we find life, meaning, and the hope of eternity. Join the celebration!

Unlikely Converts

April 8, 2015

A person does not become a Christian in a usual place, service, or prayer. There is no typical convert. In fact, if you get a group of believers together to tell their stories, all would be different and some would seem unlikely.

John Stonestreet (Colson Center for Christian Worldview) was on the radio a while back discussing Ana Marie Cox, a writer, editor, and political pundit. She describes herself as "progressive, feminist, tattooed," not exactly convert material. Yet she recently "came out" as a Christian in a Daily Beast article. On Morning Joe she explained, "I have grace offered to me no matter who I am or what I've done. No matter if I'm liberal or conservative or I've bone bad things in the past. It's not that I think you should believe like I do. I have found something incredibly precious, and it's too precious not to share with others."

Dr. Rosaria Butterfield, a tenured university professor, was clearly on the far left, a lesbian, and quite anti-Christian. After she bashed Promise Keepers in an article, a pastor approached her, encouraging her to look deeper. It was his persistent, engaging way that led her to the Bible. Her friends noticed a change as she considered the words of Jesus. "I fought with everything I had. I did not want this. I did not ask for this," she admitted. Then one ordinary day, she believed. "The voice of God sang a sanguine love song in the rubble of my world." Now she has a husband, a Christian pastor, and she's living a redeemed life.

Kirsten Powers is sometimes on the "fair and balanced" cable news channel. Earlier in her life she wavered between atheism and agnosticism. Though stridently irreligious, she broke her personal rule not to date a religious guy, and began attending church with him. She began to think that the evidence favored Christianity. Then she had a memorable dream about Jesus that compelled her to join a home Bible study looking for answers. She became convinced. "Of all people surprised that I became an evangelical Christian, I'm the most surprised. The Hound of Heaven had pursued me and caught me – whether I like it or not," she confessed.

C. S. Lewis tried to remain atheist but, "I gave in, and admitted that God was God, and knelt and prayed: perhaps, that night, the most dejected and reluctant convert in all England." Saul was a persecutor of the early church who was changed by Jesus on that Damascus Road. And the list goes on.

But are these really unlikely conversions? Don't underestimate the power of truth! Jesus didn't come to make bad people good or good people better; he came to give life, something everyone needs. In that sense, we all start from the same place, so if anyone is an unlikely convert, I am and you are.

Tax Man Cometh

April 15, 2015

With tax day upon us, I've figured out how to make both the political left and right happy. Stop paying taxes.

The way I figure, if some of us don't pay taxes the police will be underfunded, so we'll have to buy more guns to protect our own property. That would make the right happy. And if there's less money for roads and bridges, then we might burn less fossil fuel in our global warming transportation machines. Which would make the left happy. If the left and right are happy, then we should expect to see a merger of MSNBC and Fox news.

Of course this is about as absurd as me having to file over 100 pages just to convince the federal and state governments what taxes I do or don't owe. I'm glad my accountant gets it. I don't.

One time, I got a letter of inquiry from the government with a big bill for unpaid taxes, penalties and interest. It seems they discovered that I took money from one retirement account and put it in another. So, I wrote them a letter and said, "I took money from one retirement account and put it in another." They replied, "We got your letter." Then another reply, "We're looking into it." Yet another letter arrived to inform, "What you're saying makes sense. So we'll leave you alone about it. For now." What I know about taxes, I learned playing little league baseball: Even when you think you're safe, the umpire can call you out!

29

You know, the Bible says some things that I just do not like to hear. Jesus was approached by some haters with a trap disguised as a tax accounting question. He wisely deflected with, "Render to Caesar the things that are Caesar's; and to God the things that are God's" (Mat. 22:21). He avoided the trap (nice!) but told us to pay up (oh well).

Paul elaborates on the idea: "Render to all what is due them: tax to whom tax is due; custom to whom custom" (Rom. 13:7). You might wonder if all the taxes you pay are really due them. In our democratic republic you can address that, but not by making a unilateral decision what you think you will pay. It's by voting for whoever supports tax policy you favor. Then hope they actually do.

Paul offers another nugget. "Because of (conscience' sake) you also pay taxes, for rulers are servants of God" (Rom. 13:6). I tell you what let's do. Let's just pay our taxes and believe that God has a divine purpose for those that rule over us. We don't have to trust them, but we can trust Him.

God's Not Dead

April 22, 2015

If you haven't seen the movie "God's Not Dead" (2014), here's my version of a review, more a summary of the key dialogue.

The plot develops around college student Josh Wheaton who accepts a challenge from his philosophy professor to prove the existence of God. His arguments are from cosmology, evolution, evil, and morality.

Wheaton begins with the Big Bang Theory and this from Nobel-winning scientist Steven Weinberg: "In three minutes, 98% of the matter that is or will be was produced." Yet for 2500 years most scientists agreed with Aristotle that the universe always existed. Belgian astronomer Georges Lemaitre said that the entire universe jumping into existence in a trillionth of a second out of nothingness and in an intense flash of light is how he would expect the universe to respond if God were to actually utter the command, "Let there be light." So for 2500 years the Bible had it right and science had it wrong.

A fellow student quoted Richard Dawkins, "If you tell me God created the universe, I have the right to ask, who created God?" Wheaton countered, "If the universe created you, then who created the universe?" His point is that both theist and atheist have to answer the question of first cause. If you do not allow for God, a credible alternative is hard to find. The professor replied with a Stephen Hawking quote, "Because there is a law such as gravity, the universe can and will create itself from nothing. It is not necessary to invoke God to set the universe in motion." Wheaton again countered that John Lennox, professor of mathematics and philosophy at Oxford, had noted three errors of circular logic in Hawking's statement.

Turning to evolution, Wheaton pointed to Charles Darwin, who after theorizing that species evolved over long periods of time, famously concluded that "nature does not jump." Yet if the 3.8 billion years of life (according to evolution) were a 24 hour period, in 90 seconds most major animal groups suddenly appear in their current form. Not only did nature jump, but it made a giant leap, supporting the Biblical account of creation.

The arguments from evil and morality are less developed in the movie except for these two key points: (1) Evil exists in the world because God gave us free will, and God's solution is to provide a way for us to be free from it forever, and (2) without God, there is no fixed point of morality, so anything could be permissible since there is no reason to be moral.

I faced a challenge to my faith in a philosophy class 35 years ago, so this movie rings true. I recommend it especially for college students. Kevin Sorbo (Hercules) plays the professor. Dean Cain (Superman), Willie and Korie Robertson (Duck Dynasty), and News Boys (musicians) all make appearances. The arguments are convincing that God's not dead!

National Day of Prayer

April 29, 2015

The National Day of Prayer (NDP) observance is next week. Americans have much to pray about these days, but as a nationally sanctioned event the NDP almost ended a few years ago. Ironically, the secular worldview that would end the event is one of the reasons we shouldn't.

Secularism holds that there is no place for faith in the public arena of ideas or in any government activity. It attempts to use the doctrine of "separation of church and state" as a gag on the free exercise of religion guaranteed in the First Amendment. In 2011, the 7th Circuit Court of Appeals ended a lawsuit against the NDP, ruling that the President is free to make appeals to the public based on many kinds of grounds, including political and religious. Since the government is not compelling citizens to participate, the NDP is no violation of the First Amendment which prohibits "establishment of religion."

Secularism is a worldview that is now more favored by the courts than the theism worldview. It seems that the more success secularists have in removing God from schools, politics, government, the military, business, and culture in general, the more immoral and weak our nation becomes, hence our need for prayer. Our second President, John Adams wrote, "We have no government armed with power capable of contending with human passions unbridled by morality and religion...Our

Constitution was made only for a moral and religious people. It is wholly inadequate to the government of any other."

Perhaps that's why our nation's leaders dating back to the Continental Congress have called for days of prayer especially in times of crisis. At D-Day, President Roosevelt didn't call just for a day, "but because the road is long and the desire is great, I ask that our people devote themselves in a continuance of prayer." In 1952, at the urging of Billy Graham the Congress passed a law signed by Harry Truman establishing a NDP on an annual basis. About it, Ronald Reagan said, "From General Washington's struggle at Valley Forge to the present, this Nation has fervently sought and received divine guidance." In 1988, federal law set the NDP as the first Thursday of May.

This year more than ever we need prayer, not just to stem the increasing secularization of our country. Franklin Graham's prayer list includes "issues that are causing the very foundation of our country to crumble. Our moral and spiritual roots are eroding, the economy is misleading, family life is disintegrating, and political forces are at unprecedented odds. There seem to be very few leaders who will take a stand for God and for His Word." To his list, I add the threat of radical, militant ideology that seeks "death to America."

Let us lift our voices in prayer for these weighty things, not just on the National Day of Prayer.

Beatitudes for Mothers

May 6, 2015

Mothers' Day is a reminder that every mom needs a prayer, and a blessing that can only come from God. Rare is the mom who really feels up to the task. So to that end I offer these beatitudes about mothers.

Blessed is the mother-at-heart who never could have a child. May you find meaning in nurturing those that are in your life.

Blessed is the one who grew up without a mother. May that relentless longing be fulfilled in the love of family that you do have, and of your heavenly Father.

Blessed is the mother that adopted a child, for you are providing a loving, nurturing, safe home that another mother could not.

Blessed is the expectant mother. May you find peace and contentment that displace your fears about the child's health and delivery.

Blessed is the single mom. May Jehovah-jireh ("God will provide") strengthen you as bread-winner, homemaker, and caregiver.

Blessed is the mother that had an unplanned baby. May your choice to give life be returned to you as the greatest choice you ever made, next to believing in the Lord Jesus Christ.

Blessed is the mother of a sick or special needs child, for you can cast all your cares on Him who cares for you and your child.

Blessed is the mother of a rebellious child. May you have tough love, patient endurance, and wisdom beyond your years.

Blessed is the mother whose nest is newly empty, for you have not stopped being a mother, only entered a new chapter of life.

Blessed is the mother whose grown kids are not living the way they were raised, for you gave them your best and now they are responsible for their choices, not you.

Blessed is the mother whose kids turned out well. May you have grace for your sisters since, "but for the grace of God, there go I."

Blessed is the mother who has a son or daughter serving others in harm's way. May God be near them and bring them back safely to your arms time and time again.

Blessed is the mother who mourns a child for you shall be comforted. May the anger, desperation, and grief you feel give way to love, peace, and a heart to bless others.

Blessed is the grandmother raising her grandchildren. Once again, you're standing in the gap, and may both generations "rise up and call you blessed" (Prov. 31:28).

Blessed is the great-grandmother. May you be strong in body, mind, and faith for all your appointed days, and may you never know loneliness.

A Mother's love is something that no one can explain,
It is made of deep devotion and of sacrifice and pain.
It is far beyond defining, it defies all explanation,
And it still remains a secret like the mysteries of creation.
– Helen Steiner Rice

Love Your Neighbor

May 13, 2015

Before I begin this story, you need to know that it does not end well. But only a persistent pessimist would not try to find some meaning in a tragedy.

In 1991 I accepted a 2-year assignment to develop drinking water sources in Haiti, sponsored by a hospital. Living there with my young family was a cultural delight for me.

I traveled the countryside in a raggedy, diesel-burning Land Rover truck. Most days I was with my crew, working on pipelines and wells. Some days I ventured out solo, interacting with various communities and meeting people.

One Saturday, I had been to the market in Verrettes. With many more people traveling than vehicles to convey them, it was not unusual to turn down many friendly appeals for a free ride. But what I saw in the road in front of me was not that.

Two women were frantically waving their hands. They looked terrified and desperate. I stopped and then realized that they had laid a child, about 10-yrs old and unconscious, in the roadside grass and were trying to get him to the hospital.

We quickly loaded the child and sped away. Arriving at the hospital, the usual front-door crowd parted as they saw me running with this limp form. Inside, I laid him on a gurney as the hospital staff responded.

In a nearby office I waited out the adrenaline. It was but a few minutes and a friend stepped in to tell me that I had carried in a dead child. Cause of the all-too-common death was AIDS or malnutrition. Or both.

I felt helplessness and pity for that child. In time I realized that I may not be able to change a culture, eradicate a disease, or implement effective public policy. But I could do something for one village, one family, one person, a neighbor.

Christians are particularly motivated to serve our fellow man. Our Lord Jesus set the example in the way he lived, and in his sacrificial death on our behalf. We follow his example and teaching. He said the greatest commandments are to "love the Lord your God," and "love your neighbor as yourself" (Mat. 22:37-39).

As our country declines into immorality, defines religious freedom as bigotry, and devalues the natural family, it is tempting to retreat. Yet even if you can't change these by yourself, you can respond within your ability to the needs of people around you. We know God is at work to bring about His purpose in each person's life. As we demonstrate the love of God, we participate in His work. And He can change people, families, and nations as they come to know and obey Him.

I would that you never carry a dead child in your arms. But what will you carry in serving God and your neighbor?

Memorial Day

May 20, 2015

In 1983, on the 50th anniversary of John Craven's enlistment into the Marine Corps, Commandant General P. X. Kelley declared him a "Legend" who served with the Marines longer than any other chaplain in American history.

Born in 1916 in Missouri, Craven enlisted in 1933 at 17 and completed boot camp at Parris Island. While serving on the USS New Mexico at Pearl Harbor, he sensed a call to ministry. He left the Corps to earn academic degrees in theology. He returned to active duty in 1942 as a Southern Baptist chaplain.

He served in many high-casualty combat campaigns in WWII including Marshall Islands, Saipan, Tinian, and Iwo Jima. He accompanied Marines on amphibious landings through the Pacific and witnessed the raising of the American flag atop Mt. Suribachi at Iwo Jima. The Fourth Marine Division knew him as "John the Baptist." Four men accepted Christ on the boat before landing on Iwo Jima. He baptized them as soon as possible after they survived the bloody landing. The imagery of them being buried with Christ into death then raised to new life is captured in historic photos.

In Korea, he was with the Marines during the landing at Inchon, the battle for Seoul, and suffered severe frostbite while urging his Marines to endure the bloody retreat from the Chosin Reservoir.

In 1963, he ministered to the grieving family of President John F. Kennedy at Bethesda Naval Hospital. He was Fleet Chaplain during Vietnam, and ended his active duty career at Headquarters Marine Corps in Washington, D. C. serving for five years as the Chaplain of the Marine Corps.

Chaplain Craven retired from active duty in 1974 after more than 30 years of military service, decorated with the Silver Star and Bronze Star. But he was not finished. He returned to Okinawa as a missionary, and later ministered in Norfolk Virginia.

In his later years he served as chaplain at Vinson Hall Retirement Community for Navy and Marine Corps Officers in McLean, Virginia, not far from the U.S. Marine Corps War Memorial depicting the iconic flag raising at Iwo Jima.

This "Legend" died in 2001 at the age of 85 and is buried with our nation's heroes at Arlington National Cemetery. In his memory, the Navy created the John H. Craven Servant Leadership Award, given to the chaplain that "exemplifies the essence of the chaplain for whom it is named," honoring effective spiritual leadership.

I am grateful to my college roommate, U.S. Navy Captain Terry C. Gordon who is also a USMC Chaplain, for informing me about this Legend. Join me in remembering Chaplain Craven, and all who served and died for our freedom.

Real Manhood

May 27, 2015

I spoke recently with a man who spent some time as a jailer. He concluded that most men are in jail because they never learned how to control themselves. They might be tough guys, but that doesn't make them real men.

In his book, <u>Seven Men</u>, Eric Metaxas refers to the C. S. Lewis essay, "Men Without Chests" to explain that real men have heart. By that he means "the courage to be God's idea of a real man and to give of yourself for others when it costs you to do so, and when everything tells you to look out for yourself first." He presents biographies of such real men, each of which sacrificed something important for the benefit of others.

After the Revolutionary War, the Continental Army wanted to install George Washington as American King George I. They lost confidence in the Continental Congress over back pay. Believing this exposed the weakness of the republic form of government, they circulated the Nicola and Armstrong letters which advocated military rule. Washington summoned his officers and in a speech that moved many to tears, appealed to their honor and patriotism to never overthrow the newly-won American liberties. In refusing their overtures, he gave up power and fortune for the good of his fellow citizens. King George of England declared that if the man that defeated the most powerful army on earth stepped down, he would be "the greatest man in the world."

Perhaps you saw the 2007 movie, "Amazing Grace" about William Wilberforce. He was elected to the British Parliament at 20 years old. He became politically powerful and quite popular in London society. Early in his career, he vacationed with Isaac Milner on the French Riviera. The young politician was moved as Milner talked about faith. Given that high society took offense with anyone serious about God, it was no small matter when this political prodigy converted to Christ. His old friend John Newton, the former slave trader and author of the hymn "Amazing Grace," encouraged him. So he took up the cause against slave trading and slave holding, which meant reforming culture itself. What did he give up? He could have been Prime Minister, but he spent his political capital elsewhere. He could have remained in high society, but chose the cause of the lowly instead. After decades of personal sacrifice, days before his death he learned that his cause was finally successful.

These are but two of the biographies Metaxas collected, but to what end? He writes, "I hope you would want to study these lives – and not just study them but emulate them. It is my prayer that those who read this book would be inspired to become real heroes, to become great men in their own generation." May more Real Men step forward.

Everyday People

June 3, 2015

John was a rowdy, distracted high school kid in a Christian academy. On the last day of school before Christmas break, his teacher gave an assignment that would change his life.

The assignment paired him with a friend to go visit a shut-in, to bring some Christmas cheer. He was about to meet Omega Buckner. After an awkward attempt at conversation and singing Silent Night together, Ms. Buckner asked if she could pray for the boys. Despite having heard prayers all his life, John never heard anyone converse as though Jesus were in the room.

Two years later, he woke up thinking about her. He went to visit, and she greeted him by saying she had prayed for him that morning. Thus began a warm, mentoring friendship. In college, he took students to meet her, and many were impacted by the depth of her faith. The visits lasted until her life ended at age 97, but her impact on his life will not end. John Stonestreet tells this and other stories about "God's audacious plan to change the world through everyday people" in his book, <u>Restoring All Things</u>.

It is tempting to be discouraged as the culture turns against the truths Christians know, and the values we hold sacred. Before he died in April, Roman Catholic Cardinal Francis George concluded, "It is likely that I will die in my bed. My successor will die in prison. His

43

successor will die executed in the public square. His successor will pick up the shards of a ruined society and slowly help rebuild civilization, as the church has done so often in human history." His statement expresses the hope that God is always at work, also Henry Blackaby's message in <u>Experiencing God</u>.

God's servants are called to be a blessing to the cultural belligerents, and to the world. "God was in Christ reconciling the world to Himself, not counting their trespasses against them, and He has committed to us the word of reconciliation. Therefore we are ambassadors for Christ" (2 Cor. 5:19-20). All Christians are called to be part of the Father's work, even if we are unpopular or misunderstood.

In our community you will find Omega Buckner's kin providing food and financial help to the needy, helping mothers with unplanned pregnancies, assisting with medical needs, reaching out to jail and detention center inmates, and providing counseling and rehabilitation therapy. You will find Christ-followers serving in government, education, business, and civic organizations.

What becomes of Western culture is beyond our control. T. S. Eliot wrote, "For us there is only the trying. The rest is not our business." That we are here and trying is the evidence, hope, and victory that God is accomplishing His plan. Whatever the future, everyday people will still be part of the great work of God, loving and reconciling people to Himself.

Grapevines of Grace

June 10, 2015

The idea of agritourism is really catching on in Georgia. Around the state but especially in North Georgia, vineyards are a big draw, with estimated economic impact of $15 million. Viticulture has persisted throughout history, so no surprise that Jesus spoke to the ages with lessons from the vine.

Jesus may have been walking by a vineyard with his disciples when he spoke these words: "I am the vine, you are the branches; he who abides in Me and I in him, he bears much fruit, for apart from Me you can do nothing" (John 15:5). To the one who tries so hard and fails so often to live a righteous life, this is a foreign thought. The branch does no work but cling to the vine. The believer to be fruitful has but one goal, to abide (reside) in Jesus.

Hudson Taylor, a notable missionary to China, discovered this truth, and he came to call it the "exchanged life." Though full of activity as he tried to do enough to please God, he had suffered the futility of never doing enough. You can hear the relief in a letter to his sister, "The weight and strain are all gone. But how to get faith strengthened? Not by striving after faith, but by resting on the Faithful One. I am no longer anxious about anything as I realize this; for He, I know is able to carry out His will, and His will is mine. His grace is sufficient."

The believer is "in Him." What are the things that can only be true because of that, and not from our own activity and futility?   We are a new creation.   We are his workmanship.   We   receive   the   gift   of   his   own righteousness.   Seventy times in the New Testament, ordinary believers are called "saints" (holy ones). We no longer live but Christ lives in us. If all these things are what God does as we abide in Christ, how is it possible to add to them by our own effort?   Ephesians 1 is the "in Him" chapter. Read it and be blessed while you learn to rest.

Taylor shared with his friends a booklet with Harriet Beecher Stowe's words, "How, then shall a Christian bear fruit? By efforts and struggles to obtain that which is freely given; by meditations on watchfulness, on prayer, on action, on temptation, and on dangers? No: there must be a full concentration of the thoughts and affections on Christ; a complete surrender of the whole being to Him; a constant looking to Him for grace."

You know the words of the song "Amazing Grace." You know God's grace means His unmerited favor toward you. But do you know the exchanged life that comes from abiding in the Vine? "My grace is sufficient for you, for power is perfected in weakness" (2 Cor. 12:9).

Honor Your Father

June 17, 2015

What is something that you particularly appreciate about your Dad? That is the question I posed to several people recently. Listen to their answers:

"He always took me to Braves games even though that was probably not his favorite sport. But he did it to spend time with me."

"My dad was not a musician, but he drove me to music lessons and attended every show and concert. It was something he wanted to share with me."

"He is very selfless, always doing something to make life better for us. He worked a regular job during the day, then came home and worked on the farm sometimes until late. He expected us to work hard too."

"He had extremely great character. He lived it, rather than just telling me. He showed me how to live life. He was very loyal in his faith. He was consistent. In order to have integrity, you must have consistency. He was consistent with discipline, but in a calm, direct way."

"When I was leaving for Air Force training, Dad said, "They can't kill you." After training he said, "Now they can kill you." I was shipping out to Vietnam. He was a man of few words, but He seemed to always say something potent."

"Dad was raised poor. He always worked hard to make sure we had something. He showed us we needed to work hard, and instilled that value in us. He enjoyed spending time with us trout fishing and ginseng hunting."

"Dad's been gone five years now. Every time I smell pipe smoke I think of him. He was a well-respected, small town agriculture teacher for 30+ years. He was deeply liked by students, family and others because he was an old fashioned gentleman. When he passed, his students from way back came to pay respects."

I see some common themes here. A dad impresses when he has a good work ethic, spends time with his children and takes interest in their lives, is a respectable man of integrity, shares his wisdom, and models Godly living. You can't go wrong there.

Our culture says gender no longer matters, that men and women are interchangeable. The National Fatherhood Initiative contradicts that idea with published studies that identify pathologies resulting from homes without fathers. Children experience more behavioral problems, are more likely to be poor, and are less likely to excel in school. Teen pregnancy, delinquency, incarceration, and drug use are more likely. Men, you are needed!

Here are some gifts you can give your Dad: "A wise son makes a father glad" (Prov. 10:1). "Children, obey your parents in the Lord, for this is right. Honor your father and your mother" (Eph. 6:1-2). On this Father's Day, tell him what you appreciate about him while you can. He will be honored.

Self-Identified

June 24, 2015

Some of the stories in the news these days about people identifying differently than the way they were born are confusing. We all wear labels whether we realize it or not, and for the most part they help our friends and acquaintances know who we are.

C. S. Lewis could be somewhat crass, but never cruel; silly but not sacrilegious. He supposed Jesus could be considered either as crazy as a man who says he is a poached egg, or as deceitful as the Devil of Hell. Perhaps you've heard his argument that given how Jesus self-identified, he was either a lunatic, a liar, or Lord. Lewis summarized this way: "You can shut Him up for a fool, you can spit at Him and kill Him as a demon; or you can fall at His feet and call Him Lord and God. But let us not come with any patronizing nonsense about His being a great human teacher. He has not left that open to us."

So how did Jesus identify himself? Just within the confines of the gospel of John we find a trove of claims. He told the woman at the well, "I who speak to you am He (the Messiah)." Isaiah tells us the Messiah would be Almighty God and Everlasting Father and Jesus claimed that (Isa. 9:6).

Jesus said, "My Father is working until now, and I Myself am working." People clearly understood that he equated himself with God and were incensed about it. When He said, "I am the bread of life" and "I am the living water," He declared that the deepest, most basic, and most enduring human need can only be met by knowing and believing him.

He said, "I am the light of the world" as he made the blind man see. "I am the door of the sheep...if anyone enters through Me he will be saved." "I am the good shepherd" that lays down His life for the sheep.

Over and over he says, "I am." But probably my favorite is when Jesus enraged an argumentative bunch with, "before Abraham was born, I am!" Here he claimed the very name of God as revealed to Moses at the burning bush. Shocking! Lunatic, liar, or Lord?

Skeptics don't think the 'LLL' argument is very strong because to them we can't be sure what Jesus actually claimed. They would dismiss the gospel of John as a fabrication of his followers. If so, skeptics need also explain why his followers who walked with him, knowing it to be a lie, would suffer persecution for a myth of their own making.

I'm convinced of John's narrative of how Jesus self-identified as God the Son. "I Am," he said, and he still is. Identify with him, believe him, and live!
(*John 4:10, 4:26, 5:7, 6:35, 8:12, 8:58, 10:9-11*)

The Declaration

July 1, 2015

I have roamed the hallowed grounds of Mount Vernon, the home, gardens, and enterprises of George Washington. His story is America's story, how we became a nation. He did not compose our Declaration of Independence, but was the force behind it.

It was 239 years ago that brave Americans finally had enough of tyranny, so they drafted and signed a document for the ages. It was a declaration that placed their lives and fortunes in jeopardy. They did so with determination, and with reliance on Almighty God.

It only took three weeks to draft, revise and adopt, but the ideas expressed were developed over years and couched in deep conviction. The context of the American grievance was a specific understanding about freedom under God, and such language found its way into the famous text.

They believed it was time for a nation to assume "the separate and equal Station to which the Laws of Nature and of Nature's God entitle them." They were men "endowed by their Creator with certain unalienable Rights" who appealed to the "Supreme Judge of the World" to vindicate their honorable intentions. "And for the support of this declaration, with a firm Reliance on the Protection of the divine Providence, we mutually pledge to each other our Lives, our Fortunes, and our sacred Honor." The Patriots wanted the world to know their

51

intentions were not of greed, power, or war-mongering. They simply wanted freedom.

The Founders believed freedom is inherent in creation, not granted by government. They relied on a Creator God who was involved in the affairs of men and nations. Believing that God is necessary to sustain good government, George Washington said, "Of all the dispositions and habits which lead to political prosperity, religion and morality are indispensable supports."

Should not a nation founded with such ideas of God be guided by them as well? Does not the yearning for freedom still drive Americans to resist tyranny from without (murderous terrorists) and from within (misappropriated taxes, burdensome regulations, legalized immorality)? Should not our Constitution be used to preserve religious freedom rather than restrict it?

Though Washington did not sign the Declaration, he does have one. At his tomb at Mount Vernon, the family engraved these words of Jesus as Washington's eternal declaration: "I am the resurrection, and the life. He that believeth in me, though he were dead, yet shall he live. And whosoever liveth and believeth in me shall never die" (John 11:25-26, KJV). That is real freedom!

Christian Optimism

July 8, 2015

The Old Atlanta Stockade was operated as a prison from 1896 to 1924. It housed debtors and children alongside hardened criminals. In the 1950's, skeletal remains of 50 people were found on the site, the final explanation of many who "disappeared" from the infamous prison. In the 1980's, Renny Scott and Bob Lupton led the effort to rebuild the blighted building as part of a Christian ministry to a low income neighborhood. The grand re-opening was on an Easter Sunday, and the paper ran a photo captioned, "He is risen, indeed."

Providing hope and life where there was once pain and death is indeed the story of the resurrection of Christ. An unredeemed world is why He came. As Christians in a fallen world, we've always operated behind enemy lines. The work of Benedictine monks who preserved Christian truth and knowledge after Rome fell, and of modern Chinese house churches that defy communist threats, and of Christians in America who hold unpopular views about unborn children and natural marriage, is the same: to share in the recreating, redeeming, restoring work of God.

Urging optimism despite a landmark ruling that redefines marriage and has religious freedom implications, Russell Moore opined in the Washington Post that "The Supreme Court cannot get Jesus back in that tomb. Jesus of Nazareth is still alive. He is still calling the universe toward his kingdom."

Of course some Christians will embrace whatever the culture decides is righteous, claiming a loving God would not object. The Bible says "Do you think lightly of the riches of His kindness and tolerance and patience, not knowing that the kindness of God leads you to repentance?" (Rom. 2:4). G. K. Chesterton said we should not try "to prove that we fit into the world. The Christian optimism is based on the fact that we do not fit into the world."

Yet we are called to serve a world for which we are unfit. Moore's article continues, "While this decision will ultimately hurt many people and families and civilization itself, the gospel doesn't need 'family values' to flourish. In fact, the church often thrives when it is in sharp contrast to the cultures around it." It thrives because we have more work to do. For sure, the more culture rejects Biblical morality, the more likely will there be refugees from the chaos. It won't be the first time.

Chesterton explained that God wrote "a play he had planned as perfect, but which had necessarily been left to human actors and stage-managers, who had since made a great mess of it." We can be happy we are in the play, but honest in our review of it. We are on the right side of history as we have the truth, the Holy Spirit, and divine Providence. We can be optimistic that even if we become cultural outcasts we can still be part of the narrative today, and will be citizens of heaven forever.

Give Credit

July 15, 2015

Tim Tebow is back in the news, signing to play football with the Philadelphia Eagles. The young quarterback has received much attention about his public expressions of faith. At least he's willing to give credit where he thinks it's due.

After the 2010 Sugar Bowl, his last collegiate game, with "EPH 2:8-10" in his eye black and with microphone in his face, he thanked "my Lord and Savior Jesus Christ who is the reason we are all here." He then thanked the team, coaches, and fans. Seems fair, since he didn't achieve success in a vacuum. Seems fearless, too, given all the criticism he had taken.

There is a story, perhaps urban legend material, about the boxer Muhammed Ali. It seems he was on a commercial airliner. The captain turned on the "fasten seatbelt" light which he ignored. He told the insistent flight attendant, "Superman don't need no seatbelt." She shot back, "Superman don't need no airplane, either!"

The human experience is hard enough without living by the proverb, "if it is to be, it's up to me." Initiative and responsibility are admirable, but it's lonely when you look around at your possessions, accomplishments, and position, and see only your handiwork.

In the Jimmy Stewart movie, "Shenandoah," he plays Charlie Anderson, a man who had promised his dying wife to raise the kids as Christians. Here's his mealtime prayer: "Lord, we cleared this land. We plowed it, sowed it, and harvested it. We cooked the harvest. It wouldn't be here and we wouldn't be eatin' it if we hadn't done it all ourselves. We worked dog-bone hard for every crumb and morsel. But we thank you just the same for this food we're about to eat. Amen." How ungrateful, but revealing.

The philosopher Friedrich Nietzsche believed that God is dead. To him, Christianity is a hopeless quest for morality which prevents man from becoming Superman. Sadly, both Hitler and Stalin fell under the spell of this anti-theistic philosophy, and history records the disastrous results. Ideas, like elections, have consequences.

It should not be so hard to acknowledge God. But He had to remind even His chosen people to "remember the Lord your God, for it is He who is giving you power to make wealth" (Deut. 8:18). From his intricate and interwoven design of nature, to his providential hand in history and his power to bring good from evil, God is involved in human affairs.

Tebow was right. Jesus Christ is the reason we are all here. "All things came into being through Him" (John 1:3). It is a life well-lived that gives credit where credit is due, especially in matters of eternal consequence.

Contentment

July 22, 2015

The Navy veteran and retired octogenarian was a delightful conversation partner when I visited his home in Austin, Texas not long ago. As I expressed some discontentment about some small business issues, his wise words were, "You live in the world that is, not in the world as you want it to be." In a few words, the retired structural engineer had identified a component of a well-designed life: contentment.

Harper Lee's much-heralded novel <u>Go Set a Watchman</u> describes Jean Louise Finch's Alabama neighbors. "The Federal Government had forced a highway or two through the swamps, thus giving the citizens an opportunity for free egress. But few people took advantage of the roads, and why should they? If you did not want much, there was plenty."

You can define contentment as the gap between what you have and what you want; the closer they are, the greater your contentment. For the mathematical mind, contentment is inversely proportional to the difference between variables have and want. But to the point, it is easier to close the gap by moving your wants rather than your haves. In other words, live in the world that is.

"Godliness with contentment is great gain" (1 Tim. 6:6), we are told, for three reasons. We can't take it with us when we leave this world. We can be content with the basics of life, i.e. food and shelter. We can fall into a terrible trap of loving money. Note that money is not the root of evil, but to love it is. A bonus reason to be content is that God "will never desert you, nor will (he) ever forsake you" (Heb. 13:5).

The godly person prioritizes the pursuit of a more precious treasure: righteousness, godliness, faith, love, perseverance, gentleness, and faith. Will we ever have enough of these? And these noble pursuits of the heart leave neither the time nor the will to gather more wood, hay, and stubble, the things we can't take with us.

Contentment does not proscribe thrift, hard work, ambition, and entrepreneurship, for these are admirable as well. You play the hand you're dealt, but you still play to win. So perhaps contentment means acknowledging that some things are either too costly to pursue or simply beyond your reach. Godly contentment is a heavenly reminder to that earthly forgetfulness that misplaces your priorities.

Billy Graham said, "The happiness which brings enduring worth to life is not the superficial happiness that is dependent on circumstances. It is the happiness and contentment that fills the soul even in the midst of the most distressing circumstances." That contentment comes with faith in Christ that says, "The Lord is my helper; I will not be afraid. What can man do to me?" (Heb. 13:6).

Salt and Light

July 29, 2015

These are strange times we live in. Right here in the USA, charities that care for orphans and invalids, and small businesses run by families are forced to close or face punitive fines because of morals informed by their faith. Are news stories like these the canary in the coalmine? Is the world better off with fewer Christian organizations, and is that where we're headed?

History tells us that Christians have often served with courage. In 252 AD in what is now Tunisia, when the plague began to spread, residents including medical practitioners fled the affected areas, abandoning the afflicted. But not Cyprian, Bishop of Carthage. He organized Christians to risk their own lives to care for the afflicted. He seized the opportunity to show living witness to the hope of eternity. For his efforts, he was superstitiously blamed for the plague and banished. In 258, he returned only to be arrested and condemned to a martyr's death by the people who knew the good he did. The words come to mind, "Love your enemies, pray for those who persecute you" (Mat. 5:44).

Africa is better off because of Christians like Dr. Kent Brantly with Samaritan's Purse, who in 2014 contracted Ebola while treating those with the disease. His remarks to the 2015 graduating class at his Alma Mater, Indiana University School of Medicine, reflect a familiar Christian worldview: "When everyone else is running away in fear, we stay to help, to offer healing and hope. There is so much more to being a physician than curing illness. The most important thing we do is enter into the suffering of others." He recently returned to Liberia with his family to continue doing just that.

Christ-followers in America today are organized in multiple ways to serve with compassion: Caring for the poor while preserving their dignity, and challenging them to participate in the solution; creating businesses in poverty-stricken areas to give hope for communities; supporting the two lives most affected by unplanned pregnancies – mother and child; promoting the value of women by rescuing those caught in prostitution and drug addiction; educating students with the philosophy that to learn about the world is to learn about God; working for policies that bring justice to victims of crimes, giving inmates reasons and means not to return, and caring for their children; leading the way in racial reconciliation and working for public policies that support families. Christians serve to restore a world fallen short of how God designed it to be, yet loved by Him none the less because of it.

The world is better off because of believers that follow Jesus. May He grant us courage to continue facing cultural headwinds, as we heed the Savior's words, "You are the salt of the earth...You are the light of the world." (Mat. 5:13,14).

Not Judged

August 5, 2015

I put the jury summons in a prominent place on my desk. I wrote the date on my calendar. I actually looked forward to doing my part for law and order. One Monday morning casually starting the week, I suddenly realized it was today! I had one of those gasping, dash to the car, hope I don't get a speeding ticket panics.

I slipped into the courtroom embarrassed and tardy by 45 minutes. Soon the judge allowed everyone to leave except the selected jurors, and me. Summoned to the bench I made no excuses and braced myself because I failed a legal obligation. I did not want to face judgment.

Who does? Judgment usually means someone else decides if your behavior is acceptable. Our post-modern mindset that everyone can have their own values is probably why the most oft-quoted Bible phrase is "Judge not lest you be judged," especially by those who heed no other verse.

If it's true that every yearning of the human heart can only be completely fulfilled by God, then the yearning to escape judgment is no different. But finding divine vindication cannot come from dismissing God's justice. Believing something doesn't make it so! So how, then, does God fulfill our yearning to avoid the final gavel?

Jesus has the answer. "He who believes in (the Son) is not judged; he who does not believe has been judged already because he has not believed" (John 3:18).

Remarkable! Here it is again: "He who hears My word, and believes Him who sent Me, has eternal life, and does not come into judgment, but has passed out of death into life." (John 5:24). Faith in Christ means you are not judged the way an unbeliever is. Paul explained further, "He made you alive together with Him, having forgiven us all our transgressions, having canceled out the certificate of debt consisting of decrees against us...having nailed it to the cross" (Col. 2:13-14). The indictment against the believer is canceled!

Grace really is good news! But beware that grace truly contemplated risks being misunderstood as license to sin. Paul took that risk, but checked it twice by declaring that grace does not allow believers to live an unrepentant life. He explains to the contrary that the believer's identity is Christ, freed from sin and now a slave of righteousness (Rom. 6).

It is good news that God has done for us what we could not do for ourselves. What remains is for you to believe.

So, back to my story. Either the judge saw my sincere remorse, or he was just too busy to trifle with me. Whichever the case, he let me go with a stern warning. I walked into the courthouse already guilty; I walked out not judged. My gratitude made me determined to be a model citizen. Thanks, Judge.

Convinced

August 12, 2015

It is a stronger faith that not only knows what to believe, but how to know it is true. I polled a few Christians to learn what they find convincing about our faith. What follows are their responses with my editorial elaborations.

"For me it is fulfilled prophecy." In fact by some counts, Jesus fulfilled over 350 prophecies penned hundreds of years before his birth. He was aware of that, and to the scholars of his day he said, "You search the Scriptures because you think that in them you have eternal life; it is these that testify about me" (John 5:30).

"It makes sense of the world as we observe it." This refers to the glory of creation, awareness of self, yearnings of the human heart, and dignity of humans. The world seems caused and sustained by something outside of it while struggling against that which decays and destroys. Our hope is that "greater is He who is in you than he who is in the world" (1 Jn. 4:4). G. K. Chesterton believed Christianity "because the thing has not merely told this truth or that truth, but has revealed itself as a truth-telling thing."

"The miracle of changed lives." The Christian message is that we can be released from that which drags us down. "The law of the Spirit of life in Christ Jesus has set you free from the law of sin and death" (Rom. 8:2). We are empowered to live righteously. "I have been crucified with

Christ and it is no longer I who live, but Christ lives in me" (Gal. 2:20).

"I am strengthened by believers from elsewhere." The news of brothers and sisters in Christ remaining steadfast in harsh places like China, Iraq, Syria, and North Korea emboldens those who know their sacrifice. As a college student, the first time I heard my Ethiopian friend pray in Amharic left me quite aware that God is not American. "We hear them in our own languages speaking of the mighty deeds of God" (Acts 2:11). God transcends time, nation, race, and language.

"Answered prayer." Such claims can seem quite subjective to skeptics. But a sincere believer with an active prayer life does not treat God like a cosmic genie. C. S. Lewis said, "I pray because the need flows out of me all the time – waking and sleeping. It doesn't change God – it changes me." When I am changed by God's answer to prayer, I can be God's answer to my neighbor's prayer.

The Bible is not a primary proof of the faith to the modern skeptic who can't countenance the circular logic of proving the book by quoting from it. But it is still sweet to remember the children's song from Sunday school: "Jesus loves me this I know, for the Bible tells me so." That's the epistemology that convinced me.

Sweet Lorraine

August 19, 2015

It was a rare thing that happened to Fred Stobaugh after his wife Lorraine died. Grief is hard work, and out of his grief came something amazing and inspiring.

But first you have to know the back story. He met her at a root beer stand in 1938. Two years later they married. Together they raised three daughters as he supported his family driving trucks. Think of the times they lived in: wars all over the world, the nuclear age, the 1960's angst, the sexual revolution, Watergate, 9/11, so many things unimaginable in 1938. Yet Fred and Lorraine had good times, and lived full lives.

Then she took ill and died in 2013. He was 95 and they had been married just shy of 73 years. A few months later, the local music studio had a song writing contest, so he penned a few lines and mailed it in with a letter. The studio was so moved by the story that they visited him and agreed to produce the song with professional musicians. It was no longer about the contest; they just wanted to help him tell his love story about "Oh Sweet Lorraine."

Oh, sweet Lorraine. Life only goes around once but never again. I wish we could do all the good times over again.

They posted the song on YouTube, and in September 2013, it went viral. Soon Mr. Stobaugh was accepting invitations to appear on live national TV, and speak at schools and other venues. In his plain-spoken way, he extolled the virtues of a long marriage in general and of his sweet Lorraine in particular. He became the oldest artist ever to have a song on Billboard's Hot 100 list.

After a whirlwind year, his friends at the studio asked him how he felt to be famous. As he reached for a sheet of paper nearby, he said, "It's not over yet." At age 97, he had written another song he called "Took Her Home."

He didn't take her away, He just took her home. He's keeping her safe and He's keeping her warm 'til I show up and call heaven my own.

It's no wonder the story and the songs are so touching. A deep longing of the human heart is to find its place in the Creator's plan. For those who marry, His plan is that "a man shall leave his father and mother and be joined to his wife and the two shall become one flesh" (Mat. 19:5). Two people created differently yet complementary with the hope that they can "be fruitful and multiply, and fill the earth" (Gen. 1:28). God designed marriage, and it preceded not only nations, but history itself. It is good, holy, and celebrated as a picture of Christ and his church (Eph. 5:32).

Now the story of Fred and Lorraine is told in a six-part video available on YouTube. Search on their names. Seek and you shall find.

Friends

August 26, 2015

A discussion on mythology between two professors may not seem like a recipe for changing the literary world. Add a few more academics and you have The Inklings, which might have kept the world from experiencing J. R. R. Tolkien's <u>The Lord of the Rings</u> but for his friendship with C. S. Lewis.

The Inklings were Oxford dons, including the aforementioned pair and Hugo Dyson among others, meeting regularly to discuss their work and other topics. Dyson railed profanely about Tolkien's elves and refused to hear readings about them. But Lewis encouraged him to continue, and Tolkien cited Lewis for giving him perseverance for the monumental work. Perhaps this was turnabout, for years earlier, Tolkien's quiet logic had encouraged Lewis to abandon his atheism for the joy of Christian faith, without which we would never have met Aslan, the king who was not safe, but good (<u>Chronicles of Narnia</u>). Actually Dyson also helped persuade Lewis about Christ, so this was a tale of sincere friends, shared lives.

It's too bad that you may not realize the value of friends until you need them. Sometimes the need is just to be heard, and assured that you aren't the unlikeable failure you quite imagine. You come to trust such friends, which is why disloyalty hurts (Psa. 41:9). But show me friends who have weathered storms of adversity between them, and I'll show you a stronger, more honest relationship.

We're so quick to throw things away, including people. Don't.

The story of Job, perhaps the oldest book in the Bible, was about God dealing with a man who had friends who were well-intentioned but sometimes unhelpful. Here's to the friend who is wise enough to know when to shut up and listen! And consider carefully what comes out of his mouth next.

In today's culture coffee houses compete with pubs as a place "where everybody knows your name" (que "Cheers" theme song!). They call out your delectable selection by name, a friendly touch. We just want to be known. We yearn for friends because an anonymous life is starved of the sustenance of relationship, of knowing and being known. Ultimately that yearning is fulfilled in relationship with God. Surprisingly, He has made himself available as a "friend who sticks closer than a brother" (Prov. 18:24). Jesus, God the Son, called his followers "friends" (Jn. 15:15). He lived life with them, served them, and lay down his life for them.

Friends Tolkien and Lewis might have changed the literary world by advancing mythology as a genre, but a far more profoundly world-changing event was God appearing in the flesh to reveal himself as a Friend, available to all comers. By faith Father Abraham became "God's Friend" (Isa. 41:8). Are you?

Sacred Work

September 2, 2015

I was there at the invitation of my Haitian friend, Manno. Far off the dirt road, down a well-trodden foot path, I sat with a little group near some coconut trees in a lean-to of palm fronds. I was in the country to help and to teach. But I was about to be schooled.

This Sunday school class was for illiterate people, so the lesson was simply the rote memorization of a Bible verse. Manno called a phrase and the class repeated. It worked for me as I still recall that Creole verse. The text exhorts the believer to work in order to have means to help the needy. It slowly occurred to me that this band of believers didn't see themselves as the recipient of anything from me; rather their work was to benefit the less fortunate, despite their own poverty. I was ashamed at my condescension.

God created us to be productive and creative, as we are made in his image. Work is a blessing to our families and others, and meets a need of our fellow man, even if indirectly. If you don't believe work is a blessing, ask the one who needs a job. The Christian is motivated by working as though it is for the Lord himself (Col. 3:23). As we combine that with diligence, ingenuity, and anticipation, the blessing is passed along.

Since work is a blessing from God, it is our sacred vocation, even if it's not income-producing. If you consider what is wrong in the world around you, and how that intersects with your resources or interests, you have found your calling. God made people "to live on all the face of the earth, having determined their appointed times and the boundaries of their habitation" (Acts 17:26). God placed you where you are for such a time as this. Os Guinness wrote, "Many followers of Jesus today have not begun to wrestle with the full dimensions of the truth of calling because they have not been stretched by the real challenges of today's world and by the momentousness of the present hour."

All who have been reconciled to Christ are given the ministry of reconciliation (2 Cor. 5:18). There is no distinction here between the clergy and laity, for all share this ministry. Your God-given work is to bring the love, hope, and mercy of Jesus into your world, even your job, and that work is nothing less than sacred.

Was that Sunday class sacred work to Manno? Sure. But just as sacred was his work at the poultry barn for the nearby hospital, as he displayed Christ in his joyful and indomitable way with his co-workers and passers-by. If this poor Haitian Christian can find purpose and meaning in his life's work, you can too.

Where Was God?

September 9, 2015

On September 15, 1999, shots rang out in the sanctuary of Wedgwood Baptist Church in Fort Worth Texas. A deranged gunman invaded the "Saw You At the Pole" rally for high school students who prayed at their schools' flag poles early that morning. These youngsters faced what no one should: pure, murderous evil. Seven killed. Seven wounded.

Pastor Al Meredith could never have imagined what he was about to endure. In the course of a few days, he faced his own shock, rushed to the hospital, held the hurting, conducted funerals, answered the media. Then Sunday came. Ignoring the suggestions to cancel services, he preached a message that was literally heard around the world. "Where Was God?"

In a calm but earnest voice, he acknowledged the shocking news. Why? Why us? How could this happen? Where is God in all of this? If an all-powerful God really loves us, why did he let this happen? Why does evil abound?

He found the answer in this: "We know that God causes all things to work together for good to those who love God, to those who are called according to His purpose" (Rom. 8:28). He explained that believers have confidence that there are things we can know. The first is that we can know God, know truth. Simon and Garfunkel sang, *I don't know what is real, I am blinded by the light of God and truth and right, and I wander.* And that's the best the world has to offer.

Pastor Al explained further that God is in control, and can bend any evil to accomplish good. The proof? The most evil thing that has ever happened in the world was God the Son tortured and killed, but out of that came the most good the world will ever know: salvation for all who trust Jesus.

This verse is a promise with a condition. It is for those who trust Jesus, the called according to His purpose. The original word for church means "called-out ones." We, the church, need each other, especially in crisis. Jesus calls you to love him and one another.

I recently contacted Pastor Al on the occasion of his retirement. I asked for his reflections on these 16 years since the tragedy. He said, "The darkness cannot overcrowd the light." Jesus is "the Light of life" (John 8:12). He added, "God brings much good from our disasters." The fact is, after the tragedy Wedgewood membership grew by 50% in five years. He concluded, "God only uses broken people and broken things." After all, Jesus said, "He who has lost his life for My sake will find it" (Mat. 10:39).

Where is God in your tragedy, your suffering? He is with you. He loves you. He is in control and can bring good from evil. He calls you according to his purpose. You can believe and trust Him, as the people of Wedgwood still do.

Being Real

September 16, 2015

Let's talk about Donald Trump. Stay with me. This is not about politics, elections, or candidates. But if you pay attention to such things, I bet you've observed the same thing I have about him.

To say he's flamboyant and inflammatory is an understatement. He is willing to roil any demographic when given the opportunity. And therein, I believe, is the key to understanding the popular response to this non-typical candidate for President of the United States. The fact that someone may not like what he's about to say apparently doesn't enter his mind, nor stop him from saying what he truly thinks. You might call it being frank, or "real." Apparently a lot of folks like that in a political candidate.

Maybe some of us Christians could learn a lesson here. Do we try so hard to convey a winsome message that we aren't being real? "God loves you and wants to bless you" is true, but let's not leave that unpacked. It's not the real message if that love doesn't include God the Son dying a vicarious death on a cross because you are a Sinner (Rom. 5:8). It's not the real message if the blessing of forgiveness doesn't include the possibility of persecution by those who hate that you're a Jesus follower (Mat. 5:10-11).

Jesus was "real" but he didn't step into history to show us how to achieve a political goal. A wealthy man asked Jesus what he should do to inherit the Kingdom, an off-point question since it's about believing first. But Jesus obliged and gave him an impossible task to do. When the fellow left crestfallen, Jesus didn't chase after him with a challenge to believe; rather, he let him struggle with the impossibility of doing, absent faith (Mat. 19:26).

When Jesus talked about eating his flesh and drinking his blood, many disciples left him. At the Feast of Booths, his teaching was so radical the crowd said he had a demon and the rulers wanted to seize Him. He was quite impolitic when he insisted on healing a blind man by the pool of Bethesda on the Sabbath, making the rulers want to kill him.

He knew that many would not accept his statement, "Before Abraham was born, I am" (John 8:58). They tried to stone him after that one. Same thing happened when he said, "I and the Father are one." They knew he was making the audacious claim to be God (John 10:30, 33).

So you might be thinking Jesus had it coming. True, but not because of what he said. He had it coming by his own choice. It was for you. You are real to him, even if he isn't to you. The humbling premise of the Christian gospel is that something is wrong with you, and you need a Savior. There it is, being "real." It's not Mr. Trump's job to stump that real message, that's on us, brothers and sisters. Believe it!

Dangerous Faith

September 23, 2015

We just passed the anniversary of the 9/11 terrorism that took American lives in New York, Washington D. C., and Pennsylvania in 2001. The same religious belief that inspired those events is still wreaking havoc in Syria and Iraq, forcing thousands of refugees to flee the murder and mayhem. As evil as this is, some people incredibly equate Christianity as similarly dangerous.

Markos Moulitsas, founder of DailyKos.com wrote a book in which he made the case that Christians are the "American Taliban." He makes a sweeping moral equivalence between the terroristic tactics of radical Islamists, and Christians embracing the morals Jesus taught and inviting people to believe Him.

Shepard Smith of Fox News apparently bought into this "haters" theme more than once on-air. He chastised and mocked Christians as hypocritical for promoting traditional morality while rejecting Sharia Law as not applicable under the U.S. Constitution. Apparently that makes us dangerous and intolerant.

Laura Miller, founder of Salon.com, and columnist for The New York Times Book Review was appalled to realize that C. S. Lewis' Narnia books are Christian allegory. She apparently concluded that the Christian themes that permeate the books are subversive. Perhaps she can't reconcile her love of the story as a child with her rejection

75

of Christ as an adult, but does that make the beloved Narnia author dangerous?

Richard Dawkins is a secular atheist author. He rejects a god who is "a petty, unjust, unforgiving control freak; a vindictive, bloodthirsty ethnic cleanser; a misogynistic, homophobic, racist, infanticidal... capriciously malevolent bully" (The God Delusion). I'm happy to confirm that the Christian faith knows of no such boogie man. Mr. Dawkins' writing projects and speaking tours have the fervor of an evangelist trying to deliver his audience from what he sees as the dangerous trap of faith.

Is Christianity dangerous because it teaches self-sacrifice? What kind of world would it be if the greatest value was self-preservation or survival of the fittest? Is it dangerous because we recognize that our innate sense of morality must come from a Lawgiver that yearns for humanity to know Him despite our immorality?

Actually Christianity should be dangerous. The love of Jesus is a life-changing threat to selfishness, hatred, and evil. Faith in Christ is a threat to life without meaning, sin without forgiveness, religion without relationship. It attacks fear, anger, and loneliness. We can only hope that it leads to an epidemic of hope and healing of the human heart.

Jesus said, "Come to Me, all who are weary and heavy-laden, and I will give you rest" (Mat. 11:28). Sounds dangerous.

Georgia History

September 30, 2015

Savannah is a beautifully preserved monument to the history of Georgia's founding. I renewed my interest recently by reviewing <u>Colonial Georgia and the Creeks: Anglo-Indian Diplomacy on the Southern Frontier, 1733-1763</u> by Dr. John Juricek, Professor Emeritus of History at Emory University. As a native Georgian and a Christian, I find aspects of colonial history noteworthy and challenging.

In 1732, General James Oglethorpe was among the Trustees receiving a charter from King George II for the new colony. Dr. Juricek explains that Georgia was intended to be "a refuge for the disadvantaged of England and Europe" and "where enslavement of blacks and exploitation of Indians were prohibited." These great goals reflect Christian compassion and decency, if only our forebears had met them.

South Carolina provided generous support for the new colony, welcoming a buffer from the Creek Indians. The Creeks were familiar with Europeans, had established trading partnerships, and some had intermarried with the English. In 1733, at the recommendation of South Carolina Governor Robert Johnson, Oglethorpe selected Yamacraw Bluff to settle the first colonists and establish the City of Savannah. This was the location of an existing trading post and Indian settlement along the banks of the Savannah River. Chief Tomochichi willingly offered land for the colony. From this initial encounter, Oglethorpe reported to the Trustees that the Indians wanted "to be instructed in the Christian Religion," an admirable but overly optimistic idea.

The final authority for a land treaty rested with the various tribes of the Lower Creek nation which occupied what is now South Georgia and Alabama. During treaty talks, one chief said to the English, "I knew you were sent by Him who lives in Heaven, to teach us Indians Wisdom." Perhaps these religious sentiments led Oglethorpe in 1735 to extend an invitation to John and Charles Wesley to serve in the new colony.

The Wesleys and George Whitefield were known as Methodists and were early founders of the evangelical movement. In 1738, Whitefield followed his friends to Savannah and served the church previously led by John Wesley. In 1740, this new Georgian was instrumental in the "Great Awakening," a spiritual renewal among the colonies that soon spread to England.

Today's challenge for Christians in Georgia is no different than in colonial days. Even if some of their efforts were flawed, the early Georgians accepted Jesus' commission to "go and make disciples of all the nations, baptizing them in the name of the Father and the Son and the Holy Spirit, teaching them to observe all that I commanded you" (Mat. 28:19-20). Georgia is still a mission field as the world comes to us.

Prophecy

October 7, 2015

A lunar eclipse when the moon is nearest the earth takes on shades of red. Such a "blood moon" happened last month and we're still here to tell about it! Anyway, I'm not sure what to make of some of the speculative interpretations of Biblical prophecy linked to this phenomenon, but I wouldn't want to "throw the baby out with the bathwater." Prophetic writings in the Bible are instructive.

The Hebrew prophet Joel wrote, and it's repeated in Revelations, that the moon becomes like blood before the Day of the Lord comes. If this refers to a lunar tetrad, the world has experienced eight since New Testament times. Peter preached that Joel's prophecy was fulfilled at Pentecost. I tend to think these celestial sightings are more like Noah's rainbow, a reminder of a promise of more fulfillment to come. "With the Lord one day is like a thousand years" (2 Pet. 3:8) implies that God is biding his time, but not in silence.

With the perspective of history, we can witness the veracity of Biblical prophecies. Isaiah wrote (700 BC) that the Messiah would be from Galilee, and would be God Himself. He added that the Messiah would be a suffering servant, smitten and pierced for our sin. Micah, a contemporary of Isaiah, claimed that the eternal ruler in Israel would be from Bethlehem. Daniel prophesied (530 BC) that the Messiah would be "cut off" and then the sanctuary would be destroyed. David (1000 BC) predicted that the Messiah would not stay dead.

These and over 300 detailed, ancient, Hebrew prophecies were fulfilled by Jesus Christ. Born in Bethlehem and raised in Galilee, He was smitten, pierced, and killed. His resurrection from the dead proves his claim to be God. A few years later in 70 AD, history records the destruction of the temple in Jerusalem.

Given that astounding accuracy, it is tantalizing to use the Bible to interpret current events. For example, Ezekiel (580 BC) describes an apocalyptic scene where God delivers Israel from an attack from surrounding lands which some correlate to today's growing alliance between Russia, Iran, and Iraq. We could occupy ourselves connecting the dots here, but I find more peace in looking at prophecy through the lens Jesus provided us. He listed plenty of end times signs to observe, many happening even now. But He was not dropping clues so we could sleuth the day or hour, but to urge us to prepare as though His return is imminent (Mat. 24:44).

Maybe recent, unproven claims about blood moons and Russia seem outlandish, but beware the temptation to mock the end times prophecies themselves. If fulfillment of the first advent prophecies was 1000 years in the making, well, I'll let you look up the reason it might be taking so long for the second (2 Pet. 3:9). It might have something to do with you!

Forgiveness

October 14, 2015

The Vietnam Moving Wall came to our town. My generation's war ended before I was old enough to be a soldier, but not before I realized that if it didn't, I would be. My earliest recollection of it was from church prayer meetings when the adults requested prayers "for the boys in Vietnam." We may never learn the lessons from the 58,000 American lives listed on that Wall, but I would like to describe a lesson from the life of one little girl that isn't.

In 1972, the iconic photo of the Vietnamese girl with burned skin fleeing a napalm attack won a Pulitzer Prize, and changed the minds of many about the war. It also changed the life of the little girl herself, Kim Phuc.

Journalists on the scene found medical treatment for massive third-degree burns on her back and arms. She left the hospital after 14 months of treatment, about the same time the U.S. military left in 1973. In 1980, while Kim was in medical school in Saigon, the fifth anniversary of the war's end brought questions about "the girl in the picture." The communists saw an opportunity for propaganda, so they moved her to a government job in her home province so she could greet visiting dignitaries and even display her scars. But it was the emotional scars and hatred that made her increasingly depressed.

In her free time, Kim visited the library and found a New Testament. She was attracted to the first-hand account of the Christian gospel unfiltered by what she had been taught. She began attending a church and after experiencing a convincing answer to prayer, she became a joyful follower of Jesus! In her words, "It was the fire of the bomb that burned my body, and it was the skill of the doctor that mended my skin, but it took the power of God to heal my heart."

In 1992, Kim and her husband defected to Canada and she later became a citizen. With her newfound freedom and motivated by faith, Kim established a foundation to provide aid to child victims of war. Her biography, The Girl in the Picture, was published in 1999. Speaking with NPR in 2008, Kim said, "Forgiveness made me free from hatred. I still have many scars on my body and severe pain most days but my heart is cleansed. Napalm is very powerful, but faith, forgiveness, and love are much more powerful...If that little girl in the picture can do it, ask yourself: Can you?" Witness a life of peace and freedom despite horrible suffering!

I do not know the hurt of an exploited woman scarred for life, nor wounded and neglected soldiers returning from war, nor families whose loss is carved in stone on the Wall. I do know that with forgiveness comes freedom, and the power to forgive comes from God. As Jesus taught us to pray, "Forgive us our sins, for we ourselves also forgive everyone who is indebted to us" (Luke 11:4).

Christ Our Life

October 21, 2015

Gregory Peck made more than one movie about an assumed identity. That plot device is probably popular because it appeals to our curiosity about being somebody different, or how we would act if we were. Many yearnings including this one, can be traced to some profoundly spiritual truth.

Peck and Audrey Hepburn star in "Roman Holiday," a movie about a princess weary of her official duties and expectations. She assumes the identity of an ordinary tourist, but Peck, playing the reporter, figures it out. In "Gentlemen's Agreement," Peck again plays a journalist. This time he accepts the challenge of writing hard-hitting articles to expose anti-Semitism. So he poses as a Jew.

The intriguing idea of being someone else hints at the Christian life that many encounter only after years of trying to live it. Who wouldn't want to be in touch with your "better angels" or to "be all that you can be"? So we try, but sense something is still missing. Do the phrases "I need more of God in my life" or "I'm going to live for God" really express the most profound meaning of the gospel of Christ?

Authentic Christianity means assuming a new identity. Some of your personality may remain but you have exchanged your life. It's not a life that has only "turned over a new leaf." These words express something quite different: "It is no longer I who live but Christ lives in me."

"Consider yourselves to be dead to sin but alive to God in Christ Jesus." "When Christ, who is our life, is revealed, then you also will be revealed with Him in glory." (Gal. 2:20, Rom. 6:11, Col. 3:4). The profound spiritual truth is that Christ is your life. In Him, you assume a new identity! It is not just that you can be better, but that you can share in the divine, eternal life.

Major W. Ian Thomas served in the British Expeditionary Forces in Belgium in WWII, and died just a few years ago. After the War and for decades he effectively promoted Christian education and personal spiritual growth. But in his early life he was ineffective. One evening, he sensed the Lord saying, "For seven years, with utmost sincerity, you have been trying to live for Me, on My behalf, the life that I have been waiting for seven years to live through you. You cannot have My life for your program. You can only have My life for My program!" And so he finally understood the exchanged life.

Living the life of Christ means rest (Heb. 4:10), such as rest from trying to do what only God can. This is amazing grace, that God would work in and through you, so you can live the life of Christ!

Worldview

October 28, 2015

What do the Little Sisters of the Poor, Sweetcakes by Melissa, and Hobby Lobby have in common? They are stories in the news and cases in the courts about Christians who have taken courageous stands to avoid violating their consciences. Whether you agree with them or not, you need to know they have not voiced some baseless preference. It's about their worldview.

Our country is not a theocracy, but our founders believed that democracy works and provides a common peace and freedom only for a moral people. Christians consider recent changes in culture and law a direct challenge to a God-given morality that values human life and respects the design of the family.

Critics consider such Christian objections old-fashioned and out-of-step with the times. In making the counter-argument, some politicians give assurances about "freedom to worship." This term has appeared for years on the civics test required for an immigrant to become a naturalized U.S. citizen. But it can also be used to imply that the freedom of religion enshrined in the First Amendment is safe only when expressed inside the walls of a house of worship, thus allowing public space for other newfound freedoms.

The reason Christianity finds itself in conflict with culture and law is its worldview. Our understanding of what is real and true about our world requires a response that can't be contained by a building or Sunday meeting. In How Now Shall We Live?, Chuck Colson declared that Christianity is not just about personal salvation, that "it is a comprehensive life system that answers all of humanity's age-old questions: Where did I come from? Why am I here? Where am I going? Does life have any meaning and purpose?"

Life-changing answers begin with the Biblical revelation that Jesus is "the image of the invisible God," that "by Him all things were created," and "in Him all things hold together." The Father chose to "reconcile all things to himself" through the Son. (Col. 1). So either God is Creator, or man is. If God is, then how can believers contradict Him by redefining or revaluing what God created? If "all things" includes culture and the world He created, should we not seek ways to join in that divine reconciliation? Our example is Jesus, a friend to sinners. Our challenge is to love people and work to reconcile a fallen world with its Creator. Here we stand; we can do no other.

Christianity is a coherent worldview unlike any other. It is believed privately, but lived publically. The church house doesn't contain it and the courthouse doesn't frighten it. C. S. Lewis wrote, "I believe in Christianity as I believe the sun has risen: not only because I see it, but because by it I see everything else." Such a worldview offers plausible answers to ultimate questions and, as we have seen in the news, it inspires courage to stand for what is true.

Amazing Grace

November 4, 2015

In October 2015, the posh Citizen Hotel in Sacramento hosted a banquet like never before. What happened is an everyday example of grace, a gift neither earned nor deserved. Since grace describes God's love and rejoicing over mankind, such examples help us visualize the Gospel.

The story begins with Quinn Duane being within a week of her long-anticipated wedding day. Plans for the ceremony and dinner reception were complete. But one day she had to call her mother and explain that the groom got cold feet and canceled. Since the reception was non-refundable, replacing disappointment with generosity, they hatched a plan to invite homeless souls to a meal they wouldn't forget.

So on a beautiful fall day in California, with the help of several homeless shelters, about 90 homeless men, women, and children, some in dress clothes, filed into the fancy venue and dined on gnocchi, salmon, and tri-tip beef with all the trimmings. For the moment, they were free from their hard lives in the streets while enjoying a feast they could not have imagined before now. It cost them nothing other than accepting the invitation.

This story is almost identical to one chronicled by Philip Yancy in <u>What's So Amazing About Grace?</u> He retells other true stories. A teenage girl runs away only to become a prostitute in Detroit, and after becoming sick and homeless she returns to the welcoming arms of her family. A vagrant in New York dumpster-dives for restaurant toss-outs, and finds a lottery ticket that pays him $243,000 for each of the next 20 years. A venture capitalist refuses to accept the repayment offer from an entrepreneur in Los Angeles when the startup fails due to world events. Yancy follows Jesus' example of storytelling about grace in an attempt to overcome our natural resistance to it.

We have a difficult time with God's grace because we want a god that responds only to efforts and achievements, or other people's lack of. It doesn't seem fair that God loves the world (John 3:16) and its prodigals. That love does not mean he winks at sin. No, sending the Son to suffer and die was no trivial matter, but He did it before you loved Him back. You will have a hard time earning God's love if it existed in extravagance before you were even born.

One of Jesus's stories was about a wedding feast for the king's son. The first group of invitees was unwilling, and abused the messengers. Then the king said, "Go to the main highways, and as many as you find there invite to the wedding feast" (Mat. 22:9). Jesus has prepared his own great banquet, and the invitations have been issued. It is an invitation to receive His gift of love. And that, friend, is amazing grace.

Ragamuffin

November 11, 2015

The movie "Ragamuffin" begins with a raspy voice declaring, "I am utterly convinced that on judgment day, the Lord Jesus will ask one question and only one question: Did you believe that I loved you?" The movie is about Rich Mullins, the Christian songwriter and artist who called himself a "ragamuffin."

Perhaps you are familiar with some of these songs composed by Mullins: "Awesome God," "Sing Your Praise to the Lord," "Step By Step," "Verge of a Miracle." You might suppose that the writer of these insightful pieces would be a person unscarred by the hardships of life. Not so.

Mullins carried some heavy baggage, not unlike the rest of us. His hurts stemmed from feeling unloved and abandoned by people near him. These wounds affected his ability to accept love, even from God. Yet he relentlessly pursued a relationship with Jesus, with as many pained steps backward as strained steps forward.

He was driving in Kansas when a friend asked to play him a tape. In a few minutes, Mullins was so moved that he pulled over to weep. It was Brennan Manning, the raspy voice portraying Jesus saying, "I know your whole life story. I know every skeleton in your closet. I know every moment of sin and shame, dishonesty, degraded love that's darkened your past. I know your shallow faith, your feeble prayer life, your inconsistent discipleship. My word to you is I dare you to trust that I love you just are you are, not as you should be." Because none of us are as we should be.

Mullins later met Manning, who explained that ragamuffins "are the unsung assembly of saved sinners who are little in their own sight, aware of their brokenness, and powerless before God. A ragamuffin knows he's only a beggar at the door of God's mercy." Manning recorded his thoughts on grace in <u>The Ragamuffin Gospel</u>. Mullins added the foreword to the book.

Mullins' lyrics for "Hold Me Jesus" are his honest, but hopeful testimony: *Well, sometimes my life just don't make sense at all, when the mountains look so big and my faith just seems so small. So hold me Jesus, 'cause I'm shaking like a leaf! You have been King of my glory, won't You be my Prince of Peace?*

Jesus Christ wants you to receive his unconditional love, even if you carry around pain and loneliness that can block your way to Him. He bore great pain to offer you his life-changing love. Manning wrote, "Jesus is so unbearably forgiving, so infinitely patient, and so unendingly loving that he provides us with the resources we need to live lives of gracious response." So is Paul's prayer that you "know the love of Christ which surpasses knowledge, that you may be filled up to all the fullness of God" (Eph. 3:19).

Mullins passed away in a tragic accident in 1997. Manning died in 2013 at the age of 78. But their message resonates that Jesus even loves ragamuffins. The movie is on Netflix.

Terrorist No More

November 18, 2015

Mrs. Fowler and I attended a weekend conference last month. After locating our assigned table, I enjoyed making the acquaintance of a rather soft-spoken pastor. I was later shocked to learn that in an earlier time I would not have wanted to be in the same room, much less share a meal with him.

I had met Dr. Tom Tarrants. He is on staff at the C. S. Lewis Institute in Washington D. C. I was interested in his speaking and writing activities, and he was interested to learn that I pastor a house church. He being about ten years my senior, I asked for and received his counsel on a few matters. But that's not the end of it.

The next morning, I met a young man who also works in the D. C. area. I mentioned my dinner companion, and learned that he knows Dr. Tarrants quite well. Then, I thought jokingly, he said, "So, you had dinner with a terrorist." He wasn't joking.

In 1967, J. Edgar Hoover's FBI had Tarrants on the Ten Most Wanted list. As a member of the White Knights of the KKK, he was known to be involved in multiple bombings and crimes of terror. He was "the most dangerous man in Mississippi." The FBI nearly killed him during his capture in the act of placing a bomb. He earned a prison sentence, but escaped. After his recapture, and during his years of solitary confinement, he read the Bible, and came to know the real Jesus. His demeanor was different, the hatred was gone, and he began to make amends even to the agents that captured him. Many were so moved by the sincerity of his message that they too placed their faith in the One who changes hearts.

Later that morning, I stepped into the meeting room set for 500 people, and saw Dr. Tarrants. I was still wide-eyed at my startling discovery. I asked him if I could present his story to you, dear reader. Giving his reluctant approval, he said, "It's all about God's grace." God can redeem and change even a hate-filled, domestic terrorist. Tarrants has testified, "I found myself knowing I needed the grace of God and the forgiveness of my sins. For the first time, what Jesus did on the cross became really precious and personally important to me."

Tarrants was an angry criminal who needed rescuing. But a nice, decent person needs a Savior just as much. "All have sinned," which surely we already knew (Rom. 3:23). There are no degrees of being a Christian; either you are, or aren't. Faith in Jesus Christ changes your being. "If anyone is in Christ, he is a new creature; the old things passed away" (2 Cor. 5:17).

Tom Tarrants is a trophy of God's grace, a new creature indeed. One evidence that God exists and the gospel of Christ is true is a changed life. May your life testify to that truth.

Thankful Poll

November 25, 2015

Last week I asked a few people to explore their thankfulness by answering a few questions. Perhaps the same questions might spur a discussion around your table, so here they are, followed by some thoughtful responses to my poll:

What do you wish you had been more thankful for in the past?

What do you wish others were more thankful for now?

What has happened recently that has made you more thankful for some aspect of God's character?

An expectant couple, told by doctor they lost the baby, describing the last test: "The ultrasound revealed a perfectly healthy baby! We were and still are overjoyed! There were a lot of people praying for us. We sincerely believe it was God's love that caused the miracle to take place."

A person with a large, loving family: "There are special people that are in heaven now that I wish I had one more day with. I'd spend it telling them how much they mean to me and how thankful I am for them, their love, their influence on my life."

A great-grandmother: "My days of climbing ladders, changing lightbulbs, sitting cross legged on the floor, taking long walks, spending hours shopping are over. I wish I'd thanked God more often for painless days and nights, the abilities to do many things that I took for granted physically."

A career educator: "I wish the children I work with had a better appreciation for all they have: every new gadget, the latest clothes, nice vacations. But since that is all they have ever known, they have little appreciation for it. There is such a spirit of entitlement."

A voter: "I wish others were more thankful for leaders who have real, unapologetic honesty. I'm talking about people speaking the truth, standing up for what they believe."

A businessman: "Due to events in my family, as well as the tragedies by ISIS recently, I know that God is sovereign over the affairs of humans and that he can work all things together for good, as in the life of Joseph (in Genesis)."

Someone raised with a strident view of God: "I am thankful for God's grace and forgiveness. I have always felt so unworthy and unloved that it is so amazing to me now that I really GET it. God loves me no matter what!"

A parent: "My child's daily tantrums and disobedience at times is overwhelming but has made me realize how much grace and patience our Heavenly Father has with us continuously."

As you ponder life's blessings, you have One to thank. "Every good gift and every perfect gift is from above, coming down from the Father of lights" (Jas. 1:17). "O give thanks unto the Lord for He is good, for his mercy endures forever" (Psa. 118:29).

Happy Thanksgiving!

Christmas Home

December 2, 2015

It's that time of year when the giving of thanks leans into the giving of Christmas. If for you that means gift-buying dread, travel concerns, or awkward parties, I'd like to offer you something that might freshen and deepen your thoughts about Christmas.

G. K. Chesterton was a dominating British writer in the early 20th century. He was a journalist, art critic, crime novelist, and defender of the Christian faith. T. S. Eliot described his poetry as "first-rate journalistic balladry" having observed a connection to common themes of life.

Among his many works we find a Christmas poem. In it, which I only excerpt below due to brevity's demands, he explores homecomings. Before reading, it helps to settle into the soft memories of your own sweet homecomings, such as that time, amidst the world's rudeness and triviality, you escaped back to family, home, and hearth to recover some peace. Wasn't it a time of rest and a place of belonging with loved ones, good memories, and the blessing of Mom's cooking? Now you're ready for "The House of Christmas":

There fared a mother driven forth, out of an inn to roam;
In the place where she was homeless, all men are at home.

Here we have battle and blazing eyes,
And chance and honor and high surprise,

But our homes are under miraculous skies
Where the yule tale was begun.

A Child in a foul stable where the beasts feed and foam,
Only where He was homeless are you and I at home.

To an open house in the evening, Home shall men come,
To an older place than Eden and a taller town than Rome.
To the end of the way of the wandering star,
To the things that cannot be and that are,
To the place where God was homeless and all men are at
home.

Chesterton connects the idea of home to that great mystery of God's coming in the flesh, not to house or inn, but a foul stable of beasts. Yet in that non-home, you find the home that a searching soul seeks. Looking into that scene, you see that God reveals His love as an Innocent who would take away your sins. At once, Bethlehem acknowledges the battle and blazing harshness of life, but offers an open door, a journey's end, and eternity's miracle. "Come to me," Jesus said, "and I will give you rest," an invitation to come home (Mat. 11:28).

Chesterton once said that "joy is the gigantic secret of the Christian." As the angel expressed to the shepherds, "Do not be afraid; for behold, I bring you good news of great joy which will be for all the people." In today's fearful world, all need good news and great joy, a Christmas gift meant especially for you.

John's Christmas Story

December 9, 2015

I thought a pastor friend of mine had stepped out of his usual humble character, at least during his introductory statement. Anyone without a working knowledge of the Gospels probably fell for it.

He began his comments, "Tonight I will recite from memory the entire Christmas story..." "What is he doing?" I wondered privately. He continued, "...from the Gospel according to John." I suddenly realized the prank, but stifled a laugh. He stepped back from the podium, clasped his hands behind his back and glanced heavenward in a grandiose pose, caught a chest full of air so as to recite paragraphs without inhaling, and pausing for comedic timing, said, "The Word became flesh!" Which is John's entire Christmas story in four words.

It's true that John left the details to Dr. Luke and Tax Collector Matthew. But what a profound albeit brief account of the events long ago in the little town of Bethlehem! John starts his Gospel by agreeing with the ancient Greeks that the unity, coherence, and meaning of the universe is found in a divine power called Logos, i.e. Word. He adds that the Word has no origin, is the agency of creation, and is the life and Light of humanity. Then his startling Nativity narrative that the Word came to Earth as a human! He is describing Jesus, the Jewish Messiah, the Lamb of God who takes away the sin of the world.

The lack of angelic visitations, no-vacancy inns, and mysterious Magi from afar make that simple Christmas account in John easy to miss. That's no tragedy, as long as you don't miss the meaning of it. Max Lucado imagined that even eyewitnesses may have missed the blessed event's meaning. "The merchants are unaware that God has visited their planet. The innkeeper would never believe that he had just sent God into the cold. And the people would scoff at anyone who told them the Messiah lay in the arms of a teenager on the outskirts of their village. They were all too busy to consider the possibility. Those who missed His Majesty's arrival that night missed it not because of evil acts or malice; no, they missed it because they simply weren't looking." Lucado expounds John's phrase, "The world did not know him." Is the world looking, knowing yet?

The simplest telling of the Christmas story is in this final Gospel. God the Son was with the Father in the beginning, and He took on humanity so He could take on the cross. His Christmas gift is for anyone who receives Him and believes in His name, to be reborn as a child of God by His grace. See for yourself in John chapter 1, the short version.

Changed Lyrics

December 16, 2015

"Have Yourself a Merry Little Christmas" is considered by some to be the greatest Christmas song of all-time. What you may not know about the composer is really quite a story.

Hugh Martin was born in 1914, the son of an architect in Birmingham, Alabama. At his mother's urging, he developed his talent and followed his dream into the world of show business. He eventually moved to California where he became part of the Hollywood's Golden Age, working with stars like Judy Garland, Gene Kelly, and Debbie Reynolds.

Martin is best known for the 1944 musical "Meet Me In St. Louis" in which Judy Garland performed his famous Christmas composition. The lyrics are sentimental, hoping away troubles and pining for friends. The song maintains its secular theme, even with the line *We all will be together if the fates allow*, which works for Hollywood, but is a hollow hope.

The young composer went on to enlist during WWII, serving the troops as an entertainer. After the war, he returned to his show business career, but soon began to suffer bouts of depression as the Golden Age waned.

In 1974 at the age of 60, he entered a hospital for physical and psychological treatment. A fellow patient explained and demonstrated the Christian gospel to Martin, and he experienced a decisive conversion to

Christ! He said that his life had been self-centered and he had "hit rock bottom. God had to bring it to my attention that I was not all I thought I was." After his recovery, his career changed as he began to work in gospel music.

That's not all that changed. In 2001 he wrote new lyrics for his Christmas tune, including these:

Have yourself a blessed little Christmas,
Christ the King is born.
Tell the world we celebrate the Savior's birth.
Let us gather to sing to Him,
and to bring to Him our praise."

Quite a departure from whatever the "fates" might allow. Joni Eareckson Tada recorded this version with Martin for her radio program in 2008.

The first part of Martin's life is characterized by success, dazzle, and awards, but that lifestyle didn't bring real happiness as his troubles were not "out of sight." That was not the final stanza of his life's lyrics as he experienced a changed life complete with new lyrics. An authentic encounter with Jesus Christ has that effect, giving hope for the most lost, depressed, ruined person. The Psalmist calls, "Sing to Him a new song!" (Psa. 33:2-3). Welcoming the coming of the Savior brings the gift of a new song to sing, new lyrics to live.

Before Martin died in 2011 at age 96, he said, "It was my pleasure to talk about Jesus. There's nothing I'd rather do." I share his sentiments and his wish that you "have yourself a blessed little Christmas!"

A Child is Born

December 23, 2015

Charles Jennens helped make his friend rather famous. That wasn't his intent, as he had far loftier goals for what he wanted them to produce together.

As a devout Christian, Jennens was concerned about cultural trends. The questions raised by opinion-makers challenging traditional values were causing church goers and even church leaders to doubt the authority of the Bible and the truth claims made by and about Jesus Christ.

So Jennens approached his German friend, an entertainer, with a lofty idea. He wanted to use the medium of popular music to present lyrics based on the King James Bible, to tell the story of Jesus in an uplifting and powerful way in secular settings. He reasoned that an authentic Christian voice was needed to counter the cultural mood of the day. So with Jennens selecting the words and his friend composing the music (in just 24 days), they produced a work that accomplished their purpose, and unintentionally ensured that history would never forget them.

The year was 1741. The friend was George Handel. The work they produced was an English-language, three-part oratorio called "Messiah." Now you know the rest of the story (regards to Paul Harvey!).

Handel originally intended the "Messiah" for Easter, as he introduced the new oratorio near that holiday in 1742 in Dublin.   However today it is more associated with Christmas because Part 1 emphasizes fulfilled prophecy of the Messiah's first Advent. A Chorus in Part 1 presents this profound text:

For unto us a child is born, unto us a son is given,
and the government shall be upon His shoulder;
and His name shall be called Wonderful, Counselor,
The mighty God, The everlasting Father, The Prince of
Peace. (Isa. 9:6)

The more famous Hallelujah Chorus concludes Part 2 amidst a selection of texts about the crucifixion, resurrection, second advent, and the day of judgment. Enlightenment philosophers in the 18th century challenged these truths and the deity of Christ as do skeptics today, mythologizing the idea of a Creator born into His creation. Yet without Bethlehem, there is no Calvary; if no Calvary the empty tomb is empty of meaning. "He had to be made like His brethren in all things, so that He might become a merciful and faithful high priest...to make propitiation for the sins of the people" (Heb. 2:17). So, either there is a Christmas miracle or Christianity is incoherent.

"A Child is born" tells of the first coming. As surely as Jesus fulfilled ancient prophecy in that way, He will come again as promised. But the second advent will be a great trumpet and gathering, infinitely more glorious than the grandest presentation of Handel's (and Jennens') "Messiah."

2015 In Review

December 30, 2015

The year 2015 is in the books. As the Preacher wrote, "There is an appointed time for everything. And there is a time for every event under heaven" (Ecc. 3). This year has certainly seen its share of memorable and regrettable events.

"A time to give birth and a time to die." Princess Charlotte was born as the fourth in line to the British throne. The Center for Medical Progress recorded videos that highlight Planned Parenthood's profiting from baby parts.

"A time to kill and a time to heal; A time to tear down and a time to build up." A magnitude 7.8 earthquake rocked Nepal leaving over 9000 dead. The Gates Foundation reports dramatic progress worldwide in reducing childhood mortality and eliminating certain infectious diseases.

"A time to weep and a time to laugh; A time to mourn and a time to dance." A church in Charleston, a military center in Chattanooga, Umpqua College in Oregon, a county office in San Bernardino, and locations in Paris all suffered mass shootings. Much weeping and mourning.

"A time to throw stones and a time to gather stones." It appears the next U.S. President will be either a woman with much political talent, a businessman amidst his first campaign, or a senator in his first term. The stone-throwing has begun.

"A time to embrace and a time to shun embracing." The Supreme Court held that states must license same-sex marriages. Chief Justice Roberts dissented that this "orders the transformation of a social institution that has formed the basis of human society for millennia...Just who do we think we are?"

"A time to search and a time to give up as lost." In "Star Wars: The Force Awakens," Leia sends her most daring pilot on a secret mission to Jakku in search of Luke Skywalker. That adventure is breaking box office records.

"A time to tear apart and a time to sew together." PBS reports that polls show the U.S. is at a low point in race relations. Recent claims of police abuse and the tactics of Black Lives Matter contribute to the poll results.

"A time to love and a time to hate; A time for war and a time for peace." The growth of ISIS is barbaric and their Christian pogrom in the Middle East is genocidal. The civil war in Syria has given the world its greatest refugee crisis since WWII.

The Preacher adds that "God has also made everything beautiful in its time. He has also set eternity in their heart." With trust in God's time, we embrace or overcome, build on or move on from 2015. The past, present, and future form the timeframe of our lives, and per Dickens, "I will not shut out the lessons that they teach!" We receive eternity in Christ Jesus, and pray the Father's Kingdom come, and His will be done (Mat. 6:10).

Faith for the Future

January 6, 2016

What will 2016 hold for you, your family, the world? The turning of the year seems to be a natural time to reflect on what is possible, probable, and hopeful. With so much chaos in the world, how else can we face it, but with faith? As Queen Elizabeth said in her Christmas message, "It is true that the world has had to confront moments of darkness this year, but the Gospel of John contains a verse of great hope... 'The light shines in the darkness, and the darkness has not overcome it.' " (John 1:5, NIV)

This year voters will elect a new President of the U.S., but the two political parties will remain polarized with starkly varying visions for the country. It is unlikely that politicians will agree on what the problems are, much less the solutions. The world will reel as Islamists advance their violent agenda for a worldwide caliphate. Refugees will flee looking for peace; but will the violent hide among them? Closer to home, births, graduations, weddings will delight. You will encounter success, but also failure. Accidents, sickness, and death are possible, as this is the way of the world.

If you knew precisely what the coming year held, you would be mixed with fear, excitement, anger, anxiety, and joy. These are natural human emotions that can dictate your response to the known and unknown. I submit to you that faith in God displaces emotional chaos and

105

uncertainty. I'm not speaking of faith that just hopes that things will work out, or that the worst won't happen. Faith is not the fatalistic surrender that "it was just meant to be."   Authentic faith centers on God Himself, as He providentially accomplishes His good purposes in you and our world. The faith that brings peace agrees with Joseph that what his brothers intended for evil, God intended for good; and with the three in the fiery furnace that God can deliver me, but even if He doesn't I still trust Him alone.

Max Lucado says, "Jesus gives us hope because He keeps us company, has a vision, and knows the way we should go." His challenge is to "Meet your fears with faith." Since God has already considered your future, and since he has a plan for your life in Christ, it only makes sense that you respond by trusting him with it.

"He who sits on the throne said, 'Behold I am making all things new' " (Rev. 21:5). So, with great anticipation and faith, let the New Year begin!

Fine Tuned Arrangement

January 13, 2016

Suppose that you were the intended victim of a firing squad and thousands of attempts were made to dispatch you, but instead you walked away unharmed. Wouldn't you be inclined to wonder if something had been arranged on your behalf?

Such is the question raised by astrophysicist Martin Rees. In his book <u>Just Six Numbers</u>, he describes vital parameters in the universe and how they must be precisely fine-tuned for it to exist. For example, he explains that if the expansion of the universe were too slow, gravity takes over and it collapses; if too fast, it's just a gas with no complex chemistry and no possibility of life. But somehow, it's arranged to be just right.

Astronomer Fred Hoyle remarked, "A common sense interpretation of the facts suggests that a superintellect has monkeyed with physics, as well as with chemistry and biology, and that there are no blind forces worth speaking about in nature. The numbers one calculates from the facts seem to me so overwhelming as to put this conclusion almost beyond question." Notably, he also admitted that his atheism was shaken.

I can see why. Scientists calculate that the chances that such fine-tuning would happen randomly are 1 in a million billions. These chances are roughly the equivalent of looking for a specific single grain of sand from among all the beaches on the earth. Given that miniscule chance, the elephant-in-the-room question is could the universe arrive at these finely-tuned parameters with no arranging?

If it did, then outspoken atheist Richard Dawkins would be right. He wrote that in a universe without a Maker, "some people are going to be hurt, some will be lucky, and you won't find any reason in it, or any justice. The universe we have is what you would expect if there is no design, no purpose, no evil, no good, nothing but pitiless indifference." Note the absolute hopelessness for the human condition. No arrangements.

Christianity makes sense of the world as we experience it, answering questions raised by science. "Since the creation of the world, God's invisible attributes - His eternal power and divine nature – have been clearly seen, being understood through what has been made, so that (people) are without excuse" (Rom. 1:20). Oxford mathematician John Lennox said, "God is not an alternative to science as an explanation. He is not to be understood merely as a God of the gaps. He is the ground of all explanation: it is His existence which gives rise to the very possibility of explanation, scientific or otherwise."

We are "fearfully and wonderfully made" (Psa. 139:14), and not meant to be lost in the chaos of a pitiless existence. We identify with our Maker through Jesus Christ, the best arrangement of all!

God Is Fixing This

January 20, 2016

If the intent of the NY Daily News is to provoke, it succeeded with the headline "God Isn't Fixing This" in the aftermath of the recent mass shooting in San Bernardino. If that wasn't enough, they continued by calling prayer "meaningless platitudes."

After the shooting, many politicians issued calls for prayer. The Daily News intended to goad these politicians into passing gun control laws. In dissing those who offered concern to hurting people, the tabloid implied that you can't both pray and act, that God either doesn't exist or is indifferent, and that it is nobler to enact gun control laws than to pray. Overreach, perhaps?

Franklin Graham jumped in with, "Prayers are not meaningless platitudes. Prayer is direct access to Almighty God and is the most powerful tool a Christian has." Russell Moore labeled it the "Don't just pray there, do something" meme. In the Washington Post, he wrote, "For religious people, prayer is doing something. We do believe that God can intervene, to comfort the hurting and even to energize ourselves and others for right action." For sincere believers, prayer is more than just another way to express concern.

But rather than defend prayer as others have done eloquently, my interest is the difference in worldview between secularists and Christians in the background of this brouhaha. The Humanist Manifesto (1973) states that "No deity will save us; we must save ourselves." If there is no God, then prayer really is just speaking to the wind, and we are left with an idealism that hopes in removing every gun, something that will never happen. But without God, we can't even agree on what's evil. Surely that shooting wasn't evil to the terrorists that did it.

We Christians have our own idealism, that if the hearts of people are changed, gun possession is irrelevant. More to the point, if evil didn't exist, the issue wouldn't either. Yet evil does exist, and hence our prayers as Jesus taught us, "deliver us from evil." But is God somehow complicit by not stopping it? Billy Graham once wrote, "God is not the cause of evil and we should therefore not blame Him for it. Man chose to defy God, and it is man's fault that evil entered the world. Even so, God has provided the ultimate triumph of good over evil in Jesus Christ." As Scripture says, "The Son of God appeared for this purpose, to destroy the works of the devil" (1 Jn. 3:8). His work is already done but the result is not yet fully realized.

So, provocative headlines notwithstanding, we pray. We thank God that He has defeated evil. We pray for compassion and civility in a hateful world. And may God deliver us from the evil of gun violence and terrorism. Victory in Jesus!

In His Image

January 27, 2016

Four families I know recently announced new additions on the way! They are their first, second, third (grandchild) and fourth, but all have the same joy. Our natural response to such precious news affirms the intrinsic value of human beings, though these babies have accomplished nothing yet. They just exist, safe and oblivious inside their moms.

We love, care for, train, and educate children because of a truth expressed by the Psalmist, "You formed my inward parts; you wove me in my mother's womb. I will give thanks to You for I am fearfully and wonderfully made" (Psa. 139:13-14). Created by God, human beings are valuable.

Why do we think of a life as wasted if not lived well or if it ends in suicide? If a tree fell in the woods, it is nothing; but why is it horrible if it falls on a person? Why does the Eighth Amendment to the U.S. Constitution prohibit "cruel and unusual punishments"? Why do the Geneva Conventions protect prisoners of war, regardless of how they fought? The answer is that human beings have intrinsic value and we know that, even if we refuse to admit it.

Where does this value come from? Scripture says, "God created man in His own image, in the image of God He created him; male and female He created them" (Gen. 1:27). Francis Schaeffer wrote, "If man is not made in the image of God, nothing then stands in the way of inhumanity.   There is no good reason why mankind should be perceived as special. Human life is cheapened." If the universe is impersonal with chance origins, no reason would exist for the intrinsic value of people. But a natural awareness of that value makes sense if there is a Creator who set us apart from the rest of creation.

C. S. Lewis wrote, "There are no ordinary people. You have never talked to a mere mortal. Nations, cultures, arts, civilization – these are mortal... But it is immortals whom we joke with, work with, marry, snub, and exploit – immortal horrors or everlasting splendors."   Even an "immortal horror" has value as Jesus calls to him, "What does it profit a man to gain the whole world, and forfeit his soul? For what will a man give in exchange for his soul?" (Mark 8:36-37)

To the Christian, a person has value and is worth saving; hence we present the gospel as revealed by God and experienced in history that Jesus saves. As Creator He values and loves people, so He invests his likeness, creativity, and reasoning ability in us. To be completely human, to be an "everlasting splendor," is to connect with the God who, while you were yet in your mother's womb, created you in His image.

Forgiven

February 3, 2016

This presidential campaign keeps bringing up God. I admire the candidates for discussing religion even though their primary interests lie elsewhere. Their comments give us a chance to ponder such ideas and clarify our own.

Pollster Frank Luntz asked a clarifying question of one candidate at the recent Iowa Family Leadership Summit. "Have you ever asked God for forgiveness?" The response meandered past "doing a better job," and the "little wine" and "little cracker." But the candidate would not say "yes." Let's ponder this exchange, politics aside.

Perhaps from lack of serious inquiry, people can be deceived by a caricature of Christianity and a question like Luntz's can open the curtains a bit. A similar one is, "Have you ever done anything that needs God's forgiveness?" The response indicates either awareness of need or self-deception. "If we say that we have no sin, we are deceiving ourselves and the truth is not in us" (1 Jn. 1:8). Christianity embraces the mercy of a powerful Forgiver, not the power of positive thinking. Being forgiven makes us forgivers: It is God that empowered Emanuel AME Church in Charleston to announce that it is willing to forgive that deranged shooter.

But Christianity is more than avoiding adjudication of our misdeeds. Our infractions reflect who we are, and reveal our deepest needs: forgiveness and restoration. We are not just well-meaning supplicants that take a little cracker and wine with a positive thinking sermon to fix us. We are the enemies that need reconciling to God, the captives that need freedom, and the dead that need new life (Rom. 5:10, 8:2, Col. 2:13). By faith we are in Christ, holy, and blameless (Eph. 1:4). We are forgiven once and for all for what we were!

How is this possible? It turns on a question Jesus posed: "Who do you say that I am?" Only if He is God the Son can he be all that we celebrate in the elements of communion, which is neither "little" nor trite. God gave the Son to the world so that by faith we might inherit eternity (John 3:16). Jesus was in a unique position to offer a perfect sacrifice for sin, and forgiveness for all who believe.

The self-examined life asks, "Am I forgiven?" To affirm is to believe that "He saved us, by the washing of regeneration, and renewing of the Holy Ghost which he shed on us abundantly through Jesus Christ our Savior" (Tit. 3:5-6). An unforgiven life, once regenerated, yearns to display its new, forgiven identity in Christ. Actions reveal the heart.

So, if any of this is new to you, you can thank the presidential campaign that we had this chat. You can also join me in praying that our next President is a forgiven one.

Happily Incompatible

February 10, 2016

Billy and Ruth Graham were married 63 years when she died in 2007. You might think that such a godly and respected couple had a perfect marriage, though they never claimed that. But it was successful because they understood love.

In <u>Just As I Am</u>, Rev. Graham wrote, "Ruth and I don't have a perfect marriage, but we have a great one. For a married couple to expect perfection in each other is unrealistic. We learned that even before we were married."

They met as students at Wheaton College in Illinois. It was an inauspicious beginning, he in his grubby work clothes and, well, in his words, "There she was. Standing there, looking right at me, was a slender, hazel-eyed movie starlet!" They soon began to date, and shortly their differences to begin to emerge. In some ways it seems remarkable that they ever made it to the altar.

Ruth was born to missionaries in China, and she was determined to serve in Tibet, but Billy was just finding his calling as an evangelist. She was Presbyterian, he an ordained Baptist minister. Nevertheless, Billy asked her to consider marrying him, and waited. She wrote her parents, "We've got such strong wills, I almost despaired of ever having things go peacefully between us." Then came the tests of distance, as she left to attend her sick sister in New Mexico and his itinerant ministry grew. She wondered, "What is it going to be like after we're married?

115

I probably won't see as much of him then, as I do now." It did not help that Billy accepted a pastorate without informing his fiancé, insensitive on his part.

She finally accepted, and they wed in August 1943 near Montreat, North Carolina. An evening ceremony with a full moon, amid candles and clematis in a small chapel, they became husband and wife. "It was the most memorable day of my life," he recalls.

Decades later, he surmised that a married couple could be described as "happily incompatible." "The sooner we accept that as a fact of life, the better we will be able to adjust to each other and enjoy togetherness." Because of their differences, the Grahams learned to practice "agape" or selfless love. That kind of love is patient, kind, not jealous. It does not brag and is not arrogant. It is not rude, self-seeking, or easily offended. Love protects, trusts, hopes, and never fails (1 Cor. 13). It held them together for a lifetime.

Flowers, chocolate, greeting cards, romantic dinners are nice. But "agape" is what steadies a marriage amid the turbulence of life. Incompatibles cannot become irreconcilable in the presence of selfless love, just as in the happily incompatible marriage of Billy and Ruth Graham.

2016 Prayer Breakfast

February 17, 2016

The National Prayer Breakfast is an annual event in Washington D. C. on the first Thursday in February. It is hosted by members of both political parties in a rare show of unity. The addresses by the various speakers are an annual update on culture and faith in America.

The keynote speakers this year were Mark Burnett and Roma Downey. This married couple are among the most influential people in Hollywood. He is President of MGM Television and she is a producer, though most remembered for her role as angel Monica in the TV series, "Touched by an Angel." Together, they produced the miniseries "The Bible" for the History channel (2013), feature film "Son of God" (2014), and "A.D.: The Bible Continues" (2015) for NBC.

In Touched, you may recall that each episode had a scene which revealed the angel's identity. Downey said, "Every week Monica offered a message of God's love on national television to millions. It was such an honor to share that there is a God that loves us and wants to be part of our lives." She explained that before every revelation scene, she and others gathered to pray, "Less of me, more of you."

When Downey and Burnett began to plan a new series based on the Bible, their friends warned them that mixing entertainment and religion would destroy their careers. But "The Bible" became the #1 show of the year with 100M viewers. Downey said, "Faith is alive and well in America! The series helped ignite a larger conversation about God and faith. We were Hollywood producers daring to talk about faith in Jesus." Rick Warren once told them that the most dangerous prayer is "Lord use me" because He might just do so.

Between scenes of "The Bible" shot in the Moroccan Desert, the cast and crew read scripture and prayed about emotional, spiritual, and physical challenges. One challenge was snakes, as the wrangler removed one or two per day. During the crucifixion scene, the wrangler found and removed 48 snakes. "The symbolism of the snakes wasn't lost on us," Downey noted.

After her inspiring stories, Downey issued a challenge. "We believe it is far more effective to light a candle than to curse the darkness." She observed that America is divided by race, religion, and politics. Her challenge is that each one find a dividing line, and build a bridge of peace. Jesus guides us in this with, "By this all men will know that you are My disciples, if you have love for one another" (John 13:35).

Downey closed by asking us to pray that "with God's help our world can heal some of the hurts that wound us and the confusion that divide us." A good place to start is to see the image of God in everyone you meet.

Supreme Justice

February 24, 2016

Supreme Court Justice Antonin Scalia died in his sleep during a quail hunting trip to Texas this month. He was 79. His passing shocked those who relied on his intellect to keep this country within its constitutional boundaries. His departure adds new drama to this election year.

He was the longest-serving current Justice, nominated by Reagan in 1986. His wit during oral arguments and his fiery dissenting opinions are legendary. He was committed to the original meaning of the Constitution's text, rather than the modern legal theory of a living document that can be changed per the mood of the day. Though polar opposites on the bench, he was close friends with Justice Ginsburg, against type for Washington elites. President Obama said, "He will no doubt be remembered as one of the most consequential judges and thinkers to serve on the Supreme Court."

Justice Scalia was a devout Catholic and a defender of religious liberty. He said, "I think the main fight is to dissuade Americans from what the secularists are trying to persuade them to be true: that the separation of church and state means that the government cannot favor religion over nonreligion...To say that's what the Constitution requires is utterly absurd." Thomas Jefferson did not even practice that interpretation of the phrase he coined. Scalia believed that America is great to the extent that we follow our founders who believed. "One of the reasons God has been good to us is that we have done Him honor. There is nothing wrong with that, and do not let anybody tell you that there is anything wrong with that." I would add, why abandon what made America free and good?

America was fortunate to have such a Justice because if secularism is successful in removing all vestiges of our Judeo-Christian heritage, the unintended consequences may be overwhelming (i.e. Europe?). Even the atheist proponent of secularism, Richard Dawkins, admits that Christianity provides a bulwark against destructive worldviews. Ravi Zacharias said that what threatens Western culture is "a rabid secularism that cannot provide a basis for moral reasoning." Is that what Scalia endeavored to protect us from?

Elections have consequences, such as Scalia serving 27 years after Reagan left office. They did their bit and we do ours: pray and vote! Much is at stake this year. But even if your candidate loses, rejoice that "God reigns over the nations" (Psa. 47:8). Providence means that God guides creation to His intended purposes, and causes "every nation of mankind to live on all the face of the earth, having determined their appointed times and the boundaries of their habitation" (Acts 17:26). May the God of Providence guide this nation and as they say, may "God save the United States and this honorable court."

Bridge-building

March 2, 2016

Pope Francis' recent comments in Mexico about walls and bridges caused quite the dust-up. In his follow-up comments, he tried to phrase his thoughts differently. The politics of wall-building and immigration aside, the metaphor of a bridge can help explain the basic truth about our relationship with God.

It is natural to think of bridge building in terms of what is seen: rails, deck, beams, bents, and piers. An engineer can determine how much wood, steel, or concrete is necessary to span a river, and how much load it can bear. Perhaps you've seen the "Load Limit" warning signs. But much remains unseen. If the bridge is too low or short, water can overtop and make it impassable during a storm. If the piers are not deep enough, water scour can undermine the structure. You might say that a successful bridge safely defeats unseen hazards that are predictable by an expert.

An Expert has determined that a bridge is needed between people and God. The unseen hazard is the death that comes from sin. God mercifully gave his Law to make us aware of our accountability to Him, and to warn us of the hazard (Rom. 3:19-20). Common responses are to either ignore the warning, or to construct a personal bridge relying on church attendance, religious rites, or nice thoughts and deeds. This is amateur bridge-building:

it might look right on the surface, but it leaves the user in peril.

This is where the news becomes so good! God "reconciled us to Himself (built a bridge), through Christ and gave us the ministry of reconciliation, namely, that God was in Christ reconciling the world to Himself, not counting their trespasses against them" (2 Cor. 5:18-19). So we are saved from the hazard by crossing over the bridge, i.e. believing Jesus who is the "one mediator between God and men" (1 Tim. 2:5), and we have the joyful opportunity to point others to that bridge! We are, in fact, ambassadors of Christ by word and deed, bridge crossers who show others the way.

So who is a Christian? The one who trusts Jesus as the way to the Father. What is our purpose? To make Him known. Jesus is the only bridge, brought to you by the Divine Bridge Builder.

Trinity

March 9, 2016

The concept of God as Trinity sets Christianity apart from the religions of the world. Apologists for monotheistic religions delight in challenging Christians to explain what seems beyond the grasp of the human mind. Yet we do not explain it as unique to Christianity since the Hebrew Scriptures unfold the mystery of one God as multiple persons long before the birth of Jesus.

In the creation account, the Hebrew for God is a plural word, but used as singular. That sets the stage for the Spirit of God to enter the narrative. Then God says, "Let Us make man in Our image, according to Our likeness." So He made mankind as plural persons, male and female, in His likeness. In his fifth book, Moses clarified this is not polytheism, declaring that "Yahweh is our God, Yahweh is one." Interestingly, the word "one" is used to describe something with components, like evening and morning are one day.

Isaiah records the words of a person called "the first and the last" who founded the earth and spread the heavens. This same person is loved and sent by God. In Daniel's visions, he saw the "Ancient of Days" giving to "One like a Son of Man" dominion, glory, and an eternal kingdom, so that people might serve Him in ways reserved only for God Himself. Who are these heavenly persons?

This must have posed a challenge to the early Hebrew prophets and writers. How could they understand what had been revealed to them? Surely the rabbis of Jesus' day also pondered these things, and it was in this context that He spoke. He told his hometown friends that He was the fulfillment of Isaiah's prophecy. He told a crowd that He, the Son of Man, had authority to forgive the sins of the paralytic who was lowered through the roof by four men. At his trial He told the high priest that he would "see the Son of Man sitting at the right hand of power, and coming with the clouds of heaven." By these startling words, He revealed himself as one of the heavenly Persons of the Hebrew Scripture. The Scribes and Pharisees knew what He was claiming.

The Trinity has personal significance for us. God is love. Love requires an object, so it follows that the Father and Son would love each other. The Trinity is a loving community. Jesus includes us in that community saying that "the Father Himself loves you, because you have loved Me and have believed that I came forth from the Father." Paul adds that "God sends the Spirit of His Son into our hearts, crying, "Abba! Father!" By faith we receive that gift, and are woven into the Trinity. In the name of the Father, Son, and Holy Spirit, amen.

Gen. 1:1-2, 26-27; Deut. 6:4; Isa. 48:12-16; Dan. 7:13-14; Luke 4:21; Mark 2:10, 14:62; John 16:27; Gal. 4:6, Eph. 2:8

Resurrection Miracle

March 16, 2016

Easter comes early this year (March 27). The date is based on the Hebrew tradition of using lunar cycles to date the Passover, which coincides with the Passion events. Science helps us date the celebration of Jesus' resurrection, an event that it cannot explain.

The Bible gives a tempting challenge: "If Christ has not been raised, then our preaching is vain, your faith also is vain" (1 Cor. 15:14). Accepting the challenge, skeptics argue that miracles cannot happen because science explains the reality that dead people stay dead. Christians believe a resurrection; therefore Christianity contradicts science. The people of the first century didn't know better, so they were inclined to believe myths. A so-called miracle would be a violation of the laws of nature that we understand now.

This argument misunderstands science and the laws of nature, which only explain and predict natural patterns and regular events. They do not cause anything to happen. The law of gravity didn't know that the Wright brothers defied it. But because we know what normally happens with gravity, the Wright brothers are in the history books. C. S. Lewis' illustration was that if he put $100 in his hotel room drawer two nights in a row, and the next morning only $50 was there, the arithmetic laws would tell him that criminal laws were violated. Unless you know the laws of nature you cannot recognize the exception. If you don't know that dead people stay dead, then the resurrection of Jesus is not special.

God sticks his finger in the pool of ordinary events and makes ripples. When we see the ripples, we know He was there. It is not a contradiction to believe that God created a world that operates according to observable laws, and also that God operates outside of those laws. John Lennox said, "If the God who created the system we describe as laws of nature chooses to work outside that system, how can laws of nature forbid it? The universe is not a closed system of cause and effect. It has a Creator."

The Resurrection could not have happened naturally. The Creator who made what we describe with natural laws chose to raise Jesus and contradict the way things normally work. It is no contradiction of natural laws because it was not natural!

The only way to deny the possibility of the resurrection is to assume there is no Creator, which pushes the argument to a different place. Today scientific discoveries like the Big Bang Theory and the genetic code point to an intelligent designer. So why wouldn't that designer intervene to make himself known?

By his Resurrection, Jesus "abolished death and brought life and immortality to light" (1 Tim. 1:10). Follow without prejudice the ample evidence for this historic event wherever it leads. Join Christians near you this Easter in celebrating the greatest documented miracle ever: the Resurrection of Jesus Christ.

Resurrection!

March 23, 2016

Chuck Colson and other of President Nixon's men spent time in jail for Watergate crimes. In spite of their power and influence, the conspirators could only maintain the cover-up for only a few weeks until someone broke the sordid tale. One of the objections to the Resurrection of Jesus is that it, too, was a cover-up, a hoax advanced by early believers.

Historians do not doubt Jesus was a real person. Ample archeological evidence, including non-Biblical writings that refer to Jesus and his followers, proves it. Neither do historians dispute his death by crucifixion nor the empty tomb.

Certainly the empty tomb alone is not enough to validate the Resurrection, so consider the disciples. Immediately after Jesus' death, they huddled behind locked doors, fearful that their fate would be the same as his. What a defeated band of men, obviously not motivated to propagate a hoax! How could such a group maintain a ruse, given the religious and political power-brokers who were determined to end Jesus' popularity by any means necessary? The disciples could have simply written down Jesus' inspiring teachings and avoided further controversy. At first it seems they would do even less than that.

History records that they began to risk their lives to declare, not that Jesus was just a good teacher, but that

He is the living God. This preaching occurred not behind locked doors, but in public venues, and even at their own trials. They looked their accusers in the eyes and declared they would obey God rather than men. The only plausible explanation for this outburst of courage is that Jesus really did appear to them alive after a gruesome crucifixion and death. Chuck Colson observed, "Nothing less than a witness as awesome as the resurrected Christ could have caused those men to maintain to their dying whispers that Jesus is alive, and Lord."

Little skepticism exists for Tacitus or Aristotle, contemporaries of the time span of Biblical manuscripts, even though the earliest existing copies of their writings date a thousand or more years after their deaths. Yet we have thousands of ancient Christian documents, some of which date within one hundred years of Christ. One fragment has been located that dates so close to the life of Christ that the people involved could still have been alive to dispute any cover-up or hoax.

On Easter Sunday, Christians celebrate our risen and living Lord and Savior Jesus Christ! We celebrate his defeat of sin and death on our behalf. Jesus said, "Everyone who lives and believes in Me will never die. Do you believe this?" (John 11:26) Eternity calls us to say yes, by faith and by fact.

Donkey Talk

March 30, 2016

Andy Stanley, the well-known Atlanta preacher, recently stirred up controversy over some comparisons he made between large and small churches. After being called out for it, he offered a sincere and refreshing apology, even calling what he said "absurd." Wow, a modern case for the wisdom of Balaam's donkey!

Let me refresh your memory of the story, a humorous one if not so serious. There once was a prophet named Balaam. He lived in the days when Moses was leading God's people toward the Promised Land. As they approached Moab, its ruler sent his messengers to get Balaam. He wanted to pay Balaam to curse God's people and drive them away.

So after a talk with God who told him not to curse the people, Balaam got on his donkey and headed out to meet this ruler. But apparently God knew Balaam was thinking about the fees he might collect for the curse, so He sent his angel to block his way. It was the donkey who saw the angel with sword in hand, and turned off the path. Balaam beat her back to the path. Seeing the angel again, she veered away and mashed his foot into a wall, earning more blows. Still seeing the angel, the jenny finally just lay down, despite his strikes. Then it happened. The donkey demanded an explanation, and even more curious Balaam talked back to her! Then he saw the angel, and had an opportunity to change his words and actions, thanks to the wisdom of his donkey! (Num. 22.)

It is not just preachers and prophets that can benefit from a change of course. Probably the most overly used, rote prayer phrase I have heard is for God to "lead, guide, and direct," certainly a noble hope. But what does that look like? If God answers that prayer with a mashed foot or a conversation with an ignorant beast, might that be better than stumbling into an angel with a drawn sword? If we are held accountable for something stupid we said or did, is it not better to set it right than to double down? "The way of a fool is right in his own eyes, but a wise man is he who listens to counsel" (Prov. 12:15).

When we find ourselves heading down the wrong path, if we are fortunate, something or someone will reveal our folly and perhaps we'll have the good sense to change course. Thanks Rev. Stanley for demonstrating some humility here, and let us know if you had a talk with a donkey along the way.

Tolstoy

April 6, 2016

Leo Tolstoy was a Russian author probably best known for his massive novel, <u>War and Peace</u>. He died in 1910 at age 82. He was a master storyteller, and his later works were influenced by his personal experience of a profound Christian awakening. One of these is a short story, "What Men Live By."

The story is about an angel, Michael, sent by God to collect the soul of a new mother. Michael couldn't do it, so God sent another angel to complete the task, and Michael to earth as a human until he learned some profound lessons. A poor cobbler found Michael cold and hungry, and took him home. The cobbler's wife's initial resentment soon melted into pity, and Michael quickly learned the cobbler trade under the tutelage of his compassionate host.

One day a rich man came into the shop demanding that sturdy boots be made from the fine leather he brought, threatening prison if the workmanship failed. Needing the money, the cobbler accepted the commission despite the risk. After entrusting the task to his skilled apprentice, he was shocked to find that Michael made slippers instead of boots. But later that day the rich man's servant came with news that his master had passed away, and actually needed slippers for his burial.

A year later, a woman entered the shop with two little girls. She shared that she was raising the girls as her own, though they were orphans. Michael realized in that moment that the girls' birth mother was the one he couldn't take. He also realized that he had learned the lessons God had for him. He explained, "I have learned that all men live not by care for themselves, but by love. It was not given to the mother to know what her children needed for their life. Nor was it given to the rich man to know what he himself needed. Nor is it given to any man to know whether, when evening comes, he will need boots for his body or slippers for his corpse. God does not wish men to live apart, and therefore he does not reveal to them what each one needs for himself; but he wishes them to live united, and therefore reveals to each of them what is necessary for all."

Tolstoy begins the story with an epigraph on love from 1 John 3. In this passage we encounter what can be quite uncomfortable demands, such as "Whoever has the world's goods, and sees his brother in need and closes his heart against him, how does the love of God abide in him?"(17). We are to follow "His commandment that we believe in the name of His Son Jesus Christ, and love one another, just as He commanded us" (23). As each believer lives this Christian ethic, so the world experiences the love of God, which surely motivated this story by Tolstoy.

Ultimate Questions

April 13, 2016

Recently, a political candidate explained his spirituality with, "Every great religion in the world – Christianity, Judaism, Islam, Buddhism – essentially comes down to: Do unto others as you would have them do unto you." His point was that "we are all in this together."

I appreciate his effort to unify people. Americans could use some common ground these days. He chose Jesus' statement (the "Golden Rule") as a unifying principle, but unity was not Jesus' purpose (Luke 12:51). Oversimplification obscures truth.

One's worldview is a framework for the ultimate questions of our existence. Ravi Zacharias says human origin, meaning, morality, and destiny are the questions. Chuck Colson thought the big questions are where did we come from, what is wrong with the world, what can be done to fix it, and how now shall we live? In the Christian worldview, the answers are explained by Creation, Fall, Redemption, and Ethics.

The politician addressed only Ethics, which sufficed for political purposes, but it is quite incomplete to say that Christianity "comes down to" an ethical statement. It is a common error to presume that Jesus was just an ethical teacher, although teaching was certainly part of His earthly mission.

Jesus' most expansive ethical teaching is found in the Sermon on the Mount (Mat. 5-7), which contains the

133

Golden Rule, the Beatitudes, and the Lord's Prayer. He says to turn the other cheek, love your enemies, and give to the poor. He teaches that you cannot serve God and money, and should not worry. As difficult as some of these are, he summarizes with this: "Be perfect, as your heavenly Father is perfect" (Mat. 5:48). He raised the ethical bar to an impossible standard.

Why did he do that? Jesus did not want us to mistake ethical living as a path to God. Jesus' ethic is certainly to strive for, but our imperfections are what is wrong with the world. His fix was to fulfill the Law and the Prophets (Mat. 5:17) on our behalf through his atoning sacrifice on the cross, and to offer us righteousness by faith. The gift of his Spirit empowers us to live His ethics.

So, what does Christianity "come down to"? In a name, "Jesus." He is the only path to the Father (John 15:6). He said, "He who has found his life will lose it, and he who has lost his life for My sake will find it" (Mat. 10:38). He once posed the ultimate question that still calls for an answer, "Who do you say that I am?" (Mat. 16:15).

Mere Christianity

April 20, 2016

According to a March 24 Wall Street Journal article, C. S. Lewis' book <u>Mere Christianity</u> has sold more than 3.5 million copies in English, and has been translated into 36 languages. It sold more copies in the last 15 years than in its first 15. Impressive for what Lewis did not originally intend to be a book.

Dr. Francis Collins, the renowned genetics researcher and director of the National Institutes of Health, spoke to the impact of the book. In a PBS interview, he set the stage by explaining his worldview while pursuing his first doctorate at Yale. "I concluded that all of this stuff about religion and faith was a carryover from an earlier, irrational time, and now that science had begun to figure out how things really work, we didn't need it anymore."

While a resident physician, Collins decided that he needed data to support his rejection of God. He sought out a Methodist minister, who suggested he investigate the thinking of a certain Oxford scholar, and gave him Lewis' book. As he read, Collins discovered that the evidence for God is plausible, but he resisted. About a year later while hiking in the Cascades, overwhelmed by the beauty of creation, something changed. He thought, "This is something I have really longed for all my life without realizing it, and now I've got the chance to say yes. That was the most significant moment in my life."

The book has been impacting the lives of its readers since 1952 when first published. But it began as a series of BBC radio broadcasts during WWII. George Marsden, who wrote what he calls the "biography" of <u>Mere Christianity</u>, explains that it "originated in the midst of one of the most stressful times in British history...when there were still fears of a Nazi invasion and the Blitz bombing." (FYI, this period is captured in the TV drama series Foyle's War.)

Though <u>Mere Christianity</u> has a few historical references, Lewis wanted the talks to avoid current religious fads, denominational distinctives, and partisan politics. He knew how to translate deep truths into the vernacular with vivid analogies. Marsden explains, "Lewis was trying to present the beliefs that have been common to nearly all Christians at all times." Yet despite the common appeal, it can convince a brilliant, highly-trained scientist. Most compelling to Collins was "the argument about the existence of moral law. How is it that we, unique in the animal kingdom, know what's right and what's wrong?" That could only come from God.

<u>Mere Christianity</u> is a book for the ages. Hinting at its purpose, Lewis writes, "Look for yourself, and you will find only hatred, loneliness, despair, rage, ruin, and decay. But look for Christ and you will find Him," which is indeed mere Christianity.

Day of Prayer 2016

April 27, 2016

This year the observance of the National Day of Prayer is on May 5. In communities across America, the faithful will take the opportunity to pray for our nation and its leaders. If you feel compelled to pray and want to invigorate your prayers, I suggest using Scripture as a prayer guide, demonstrated here using a few select verses.

"The eyes of the Lord move to and fro throughout the earth, that He may strongly support those whose heart is completely His" (2 Chr. 16:9). Lord we need your strong support for our nation, community, work, family, and for ourselves. By your Spirit, move us to give our hearts completely to you, to receive your presence and guidance. As your eyes roam the earth, may they rest on us as having embraced the gospel of Christ in which we find righteousness by faith and the hope of eternity.

"Put them in fear, O Lord; let the nations know that they are but men" (Psa. 9:20). It is when a nation's leaders imagine that they have authority reserved only for you, God, that calamity comes. Instill in our nation's leaders a sense of humility and respect for a greater authority, for in this we the people can enjoy peace and freedom. Thank you that in your Providence, you have accounted for evil among the nations and nothing will stop you from accomplishing your purposes in the world.

"Vindicate me, O God, and plead my case against an ungodly nation" (Psa. 43:1). Lord, we thank you for the freedoms we have enjoyed as Americans, but we understand that these are not guaranteed in this world. We are stunned to see our culture define religious freedom as a form of bigotry, and Christian morality as intolerable. Strengthen us to remain faithful to obey God rather than men.

"God be gracious to us and bless us...that your way may be known on the earth, your salvation among all nations" (Psa. 67:1-2). The greatest blessing to a nation is for its people to receive forgiveness and salvation, and to live lives loving God and neighbor. Lord, as ambassadors for Christ may our words and deeds make your way known.

To incorporate Scriptural prayer into your devotional life, I suggest you select a Psalm chapter, and as you read each verse let God lead you to a related prayer. Let us join together in appealing to God for mercy on the U.S.A.

Thanks Mom!

May 4, 2016

For what does your mother deserve your gratitude? While you ponder that, let me tell the stories of two mothers who made it into the pages of the Bible, both deserving of thanks from their offspring.

The prophet Elijah encountered a widow preparing to bake her last flour. Her situation was so dire that she expected it to be her and her son's last meal. Elijah asked her to give the bread to him instead. He explained that God promised that her flour bowl and oil jar would not be empty until the drought ended. She believed, and did as he asked. God provided for her according to the word He spoke through Elijah. But the boy later became sick and died. She again reached out to Elijah, who pled to God for mercy. The Lord heard the prayer and revived the child. (1 Ki. 17)

This single mom was doing the best she could for her son. He owed his life to a mother willing to cooperate with God even in their darkest days. We never learn their names, and we don't know what ultimately became of them. But I bet whenever she retold him the story of what happened to him as a lad, it filled his heart with gratitude to her and to God.

Hannah was a wife much loved by her husband, but she was barren. She pled with the Lord for a son, and promised to dedicate him to the Lord's service. She explained her plight to the priest Eli, and he joined her prayer. Soon she did bear a son, and presented him to serve God with Eli. She visited her son regularly, and the Lord blessed her with five more children. Her firstborn was Samuel, who spoke God's mighty words to the people of Israel as the last judge before they demanded a king. (1 Sam.)

This mother prayed for her son before he was born. She trusted the Lord with his birth and life. She never ceased to love and care for him. Samuel would not have had the faith in God, boldness in his calling, and impact on history were it not for his mother.

Every one of us owes a debt of gratitude to our mothers for giving us life. Most of us have much more to be thankful for, and Mother's Day is our reminder to do so. If you still have the opportunity, consider offering her more than just a "happy Mother's day" wish, and tell her some specific reasons you are thankful. That should make her day happy without you having to wish for it.

Finding Jesus

May 11, 2016

In March of this year, in the aftermath of the terrorist bombing in Brussels, a new face appeared in the American media. Because he had just released his latest book Answering Jihad, both TV and print media sought out Dr. Nabeel Qureshi to comment.

Qureshi is certainly in a position to speak to these issues, having been raised a Muslim. His biographical work, Seeking Allah, Finding Jesus, documents his struggle to find the truth about God and faith. He is a medical doctor, with master's degrees in Christian Apologetics and Religion, and is currently pursuing a doctorate in New Testament at Oxford.

Born in 1985 in California, Qureshi spent most of his high school and college years in Virginia. His father, a retired U. S. Navy officer, and his mother are devout Muslims of the Ahmadiyya sect. They trained their son not only to follow that religion, but to be a spokesman for it.

But as he began to seriously seek the truth about life and God, he had questions about those teachings. At first his questions were private, and out of love and respect for his parents, he dared not mention them. As a college freshman, he became close friends with a young Christian man, despite their cultural and religious differences. For the next three years, these friends engaged in a respectful and honest exchange about the truth claims and evidences for their respective religious views.   Nabeel eventually accepted the challenge to simply ask God who He really is.

In response to that prayer, Qureshi experienced three highly symbolic dreams that convinced him that God was calling him to accept the gospel of Jesus.   Though painfully aware of the risk to his family relationships, he eagerly began to find God in the Bible.   His search culminated as he read Jesus' words, "Whoever loses his life for my sake will find it" (Mat. 16:25), and at the age of 20 he prayed, "I submit that Jesus Christ is Lord."

I introduce you to Dr. Qureshi as an example of, "My Father is working until now" (John 5:17).   Like Saul's Damascus Road experience, the risen Christ found an unlikely convert, and changed the trajectory of his life. Jesus not only convinced him of the gospel, but also moved Dr. Qureshi to abandon a medical career to give his life explaining and defending the Christian faith.

In 2014, I had the privilege of speaking in person with Dr. Qureshi for a few moments.   I thanked him for his courage in embracing and proclaiming the truth he found in Christ. I promised to pray for his safety as he declares Christ's love and forgiveness, a message that so many in our world would not hear. From this pen to God's ear!

Museum of the Bible

May 18, 2016

Something good is happening in Washington, D. C. for a change! In Fall 2017, the Museum of the Bible opens. Its purpose is to "be an unparalleled experience, using cutting-edge technology to bring the Bible to life."

The non-profit Museum is designed to portray the history and context of the Bible, spanning time and culture. The organization "invites all people to engage with the Bible through our four pillars: research, traveling exhibits, education, and a museum." Once the Museum is complete, all four pillars will be in place.

The remodeled building in D. C. will house 40,000 planned artifacts, including cuneiform tablets, Dead Sea Scroll fragments, Biblical papyri, Torah scrolls, and rare printed Bibles in 430,000 square feet of exhibits costing over $1 billion. Not only housing exhibits on the history and impact of the Bible, the Museum contains research labs and libraries for scholarly inquiry, a Nazareth Village display of Jesus's home town, and Biblical Gardens.

The Green family of Hobby Lobby provided the startup funds. Steve Green said, "This nation is in danger because of its ignorance of what God has taught. If we don't know it, our future is going to be very scary." The board includes Rick Warren and other Christian leaders and scholars.

Cary Summers became President about five years ago. He said, "There is not a major museum in the world about the most sold book ever in history, the most debated book ever. We thought it was really odd, and so we said, 'Let's do something about that.' And we did." He reports that despite the expectation that city approvals would be difficult to obtain, the Museum actually received little opposition. In fact, the city council person most likely to oppose it stated it's "the most important project to come into the neighborhood."

If its importance is to relegate the Bible to a museum, the project would be ironic not to mention calamitous for mankind. To the contrary, this museum celebrates God's Word as powerful in the lives of people, and introduces it to people who don't know it.   "The word of God is living and active and sharper than any two-edged sword, and piercing as far as the division of soul and spirit, of both joints and marrow, and able to judge the thoughts and intentions of the heart" (Heb. 4:12).

For more information, visit the organization's website www.museumofthebible.org. Just two blocks off of the National Mall, it will be easily accessible for tourists. This may be your reason to visit D. C. and see the kind of change our nation's capital needs.

Perspective on the News

May 25, 2016

This is a word of encouragement to those who read and grieve the news of the day. Much of it troubles those of us who hold a Christian worldview, but we must avoid the slippery slopes of a hopeless response.

Without naming particular issues, let's stipulate that the headlines that cause us to utter under our breath "God help us," are usually about morality, leadership, economics, or terrorism. The Bible speaks to all of these; after all, it is the user's manual for the human existence.

So many of an individual's and a nation's troubles are self-inflicted when they call "good" what God said is sin. That's confused morality.

We pray for godly leadership, men and women that are humble enough to know their place and their limitations, and are willing to seek divine wisdom.

The Bible speaks plainly about economics, not the least of which is "the borrower is the lender's slave" (Prov. 22:7). The less national debt we have, the more free we are.

Torturing, maiming, and killing people including children to advance an ideology is evil, and should be confronted. Who will advance the cause of freedom for the oppressed and persecuted victims of terrorism, and keep it from washing up on our shores?

It is hopeless to give in to the "fight-or-flight" response. To become bitter and angry or to deny and ignore the issues of the day will distract you from the perspective that

Jesus offers to his followers. He said the kingdom of God is like a mustard seed that "grew and became a tree, and the birds of the air nested in its branches," and "like leaven which a woman took and hid in three pecks of flour until it was all leavened" (Luke 13:19-21).   God's kingdom advances slowly and purposefully and someday His rule will cover the world.

We can trust God to accomplish his purposes despite the news of the day. The wickedness of our age creates cultural refugees looking for rest, provision, and peace. Our Father offers a safe place for the soul to anyone who seeks Him.

Jesus taught us to pray, "Thy kingdom come, Thy will be done." As we utter those words, may the One who is mighty to save put today's news into His perspective for us.

Organic Church

June 1, 2016

Even though churches and denominations have distinctive beliefs, most have a form common to the modern Christian church. Dr. Ed Stetzer recently blogged about a different form as old as the church itself, and becoming more common today. He has two doctorates and works as a researcher, but his observations are more than ivory tower ideals because he has also served as a pastor and church planter.

Various authors label this form as simple church, or house church. You may have heard about the growth of Christianity in China through house churches, but the movement is not limited to that restrictive country. Stetzer prefers the label "organic church," which hints at the differences from traditional church. Organic churches do not have buildings, programs, or paid clergy, but they do not emphasize that. Their idea is that less is more.

Stetzer's research indicates that the focus of organic church is discipleship. I would define that as helping believers apply God's Word as they follow Christ. He finds that in the U. S., organic church is more likely to be found on college campuses and urban, high-density areas where the cost of real estate is high. According to Stetzer, "People who are disenfranchised, weary, or intimidated by the more institutional and organized forms of church may be open to an organic church." Such believers and seekers might live anywhere, even in rural areas and small towns.

147

Organic churches may be networked, but they exist across denominations. Stetzer, a Southern Baptist, admits that he almost lost his job once for defending organic church as an authentic expression of the body of Christ. He still supports it as he expects this form of church to grow. Referring to the early church meeting in homes, Stetzer encourages believers to "cast their boat into a new sea that is really as old as the New Testament church."

An older pastor once told me, "Not everyone is a good candidate for your church." Likewise, if a person is looking for highly proficient music and well-organized children's activities, they will gravitate toward traditional churches, and most communities have excellent choices for those. All healthy churches believe that church is people, not just a building, program, or meeting.

Jesus once declared, "I will build my church" (Mat. 16:18). If history is any indication, He will accomplish that in different ways and forms, some as old as His Church itself.

Not God's Type

June 8, 2016

Dr. Holly Ordway was a young English professor. She wasn't just a secular-minded young professional, but an antagonistic atheist. Not exactly in the demographic of likely candidates for conversion to Christianity. But it happened.

She wrote about it in her book Not God's Type in 2008. In 2014, she decided to re-write it. The reason is captured in the sub-title change from "a rational academic finds a radical faith" to "an atheist academic lays down her arms." The first implied that her conversion was mostly her doing; the second, her surrender to God's work in her mind and heart.

She was raised in a family that was culturally but not actually Christian. She thought of Christianity as a historical curiosity, and preferred a rationalism that trusts science to explain everything. Christians were self-deluded as they tried to follow their morality as a set of rules and pious slogans. She "didn't know that the church offered a relationship with a living Person who would...transform you into a new person."

Dr. Ordway's rational mind began to challenge her atheistic faith when she realized, "I could not explain why I had this moral sense, and my efforts fell short of my ideals." Seeking answers, she turned to writings by C. S. Lewis and found his explanation of the moral argument for God compelling. She also read works by William Lane

Craig, Gary Habermas, and N. T. Wright. She concluded that the Resurrection of Christ is historical and believable, and has personal implications.

In the re-write of her book, she added the other components of her life that led to faith: imagination and literature. She said, "My atheist view of the world could not explain why I was moved by beauty and cared about truth." As a student of literature, she names Lewis and Tolkien as favorite authors. She found that the moving poems of Hopkins, Herbert, and Donne could not be separated from their Christianity. From them she caught "a vision of the world that was richly meaningful and beautiful, and that also made sense of the joy and sorrow that I could experience."

It was her fencing coach that helped seal the deal. He did not fit her stereotype of Christians as pushy and thoughtless, and offered respectful dialogue. We believers could use some coaching ourselves, to live in a way that surprises our friends into asking questions; to have respectful and informed conversations about the realities of Jesus our Savior.

None of us are really God's type. But as Brennan Manning observed, "Tragedy is that our attention centers on what people are not, rather than on what they are and who they might become." The humbling and rational message of Christianity is that "Christ Jesus came into the world to save sinners, among whom I am foremost of all" (1 Tim. 1:15).

Thanks Dad!

June 15, 2016

For what does your father deserve your gratitude? Maybe the stories of two fathers whose lives and times are told in the Bible will seed your thinking on the question.

Noah was a man who walked with God. He was righteous and blameless. God chose him to save the human race by building an ark to float out the great flood. His three sons were part of the great endeavor of building the ark. With their wives, they entered the ark and witnessed God closing the door behind them. It was Noah's obedience that protected his family from the flood. After the flood, the sons tried to protect the father from an embarrassing incident, which you can read for yourself. (Gen. 6-9)

This father believed and lived in a way that was contrary to the culture around him. He was willing to obey God even when it seemed counter-intuitive. He spent time with his sons, and modeled a life of hard work and determination. He wasn't perfect, but he held the respect of his sons. They had much to be thankful for in their father: his courage, character, and faith.

The Apostle Paul claimed Onesimus as his son. During one of Paul's inconvenient stays at government accommodations, he came to know this young runaway. Paul, writing to Philemon to take him back, called him "my very heart." It was a sacrifice to send him back since he had helped Paul during his imprisonment. He offered to pay any damages his adopted son had caused.

This father figure was transparent about his love for his son in the Lord. He emphasized what the young man had done right, though he had done a great wrong. He offered to help his son make restitution and learn from his mistakes. Onesimus had reason to be thankful for a mentor who loved and encouraged him. (Phil. 1:10-20)

I hope you can be grateful for your father or father figure. It is a courageous man who takes up the challenge of providing for, and mentoring a son or daughter. If you still have the opportunity, consider offering him more than just a "Happy Father's Day!" wish, and tell him some specific reasons you are thankful. That should make his day happy without you having to wish for it. And if he's gone, remember him with gratitude.

Offended

June 22, 2016

A pattern occurs to me as I read certain news stories of late. These are events from different places and circumstances, but they affirm the same Biblical truth.

Dr. Everett Piper is president of Oklahoma Wesleyan University. A chapel service message from 1 Cor. 13 included an effective challenge to love others, which offended one student. Piper's response in an open letter was atypical for a university president in 2016. "The primary objective of the church and the Christian faith is your confession, not your self-actualization. We don't issue 'trigger warnings' before altar calls. This is not a day care. This is a university."

In the province of Zhejiang, China, 2000 bright-red crosses are no longer on church steeples after the government conducted a two-year purge of the offending Christian symbol. Christians have been resilient, especially in Wenzhou, where more than ten percent of the residents are believers. The destruction has not stopped the churches from gathering, and many restored their crosses to a visible place other than the rooftop. Observers point out that there are now more Christians in China than members of the communist party, and this latest intimidation probably reflects fear of the growth of the church.

The Santa Monica Observer ran a story about a seven-year-old boy who "threatened" his school. Each day his mom, Christina Zavala, included in his lunch box a Bible verse and a note. During lunch break he read it to his friends when they asked. Soon they asked if Zavala would send them a note too, and she did. When a child told a teacher his note was "the most beautiful story," the school dispatched a sheriff deputy to the home to demand this activity stop because "someone might be offended."

The message of the cross offends people. The Bible calls the cross an offense to those who think God's favor must be earned (Gal. 5:11). For the gospel to be effective it must offend the pride that needs no Savior. It says that you are a Sinner and apart from the love, grace, and sacrifice of Jesus, you have missed your ultimate calling to know God as he has revealed Himself.

The message may be offensive, but the messenger shouldn't be. Charles Spurgeon said, "Do not let us make any extra offense of the Cross by our own ill humor, but let us show our love to the Cross by loving and trying to bless those who have been offended with it."

Karl Barth once advised young theologians "to take your Bible and take your newspaper, and read both. But interpret newspapers from your Bible." A good place to start is, "The word of the cross is foolishness to those who are perishing, but to us who are being saved it is the power of God" (1 Cor. 1:18). Take heart, Christian, and embrace the power.

Patrick Henry

June 29, 2016

"Give me liberty or give me death!" The rallying cry for the American Revolution came from Patrick Henry. This patriot, a founder of our country, was a Christian. Together with many of his contemporaries, he believed that virtue flowing from belief in God was vital for the success of our new country. Let me share some of his story that give his words and thoughts some texture.

In 1763, he was a young attorney. His father was a judge and his uncle an Anglican priest. The government-sponsored church clerics sued the taxpayers for insufficient payments. Defending the taxpayers, Henry first flashed his renowned oratory skills with this: "Such is the avarice, such the insatiate thirst for gold of these ecclesiastical harpies, that they would snatch the last hoe cake from the widow and the orphan." I wonder what the reverend uncle thought about that broadside. We know what judge dad thought: he ruled against his son.

In another case Henry defended John Weatherford, a Baptist who had been imprisoned for preaching without a license, and paid the preacher's fine. His popular defense of the common folk propelled him into politics.

While serving in the colonial Virginia legislature and in the continental congress, Henry spoke against the tyrannies of King George III. He was among the first to call for independence, once with a warning that still stands. "Whether this will prove a blessing or a curse will depend upon the use our people make of the blessings which a gracious God hath bestowed on us. Righteousness alone can exalt them as a nation."

In his final years, Henry voiced his fears that the French Revolution would tear down "the great pillars of all government and of social life" which he listed as "virtue, morality, and religion." He had become more vocal as a Christian statesman, and was disturbed that some considered him a Deist, which he said was "another name for vice and depravity."

On his deathbed in 1799, he issued his last of many appeals to his friend and physician, Dr. George Cabell. "I wish you to observe how real and beneficial the religion of Christ is to a man about to die." He told the doctor his religion had never failed him, prayed for his family, country, and his soul, and then passed into eternity.

In his will, Henry wrote, "This is all the inheritance I give to my dear family. The religion of Christ will give them one which will make them rich indeed." In death as in life, Patrick Henry understood liberty, giving final testament to Scripture, "It was for freedom that Christ set us free" (Gal. 5:1).

Moral Question

July 6, 2016

The mass shooting in Orlando was a horrible act. Before the families could grieve and bury their dead, the questions began to fly. What was the shooter's motivation? What laws and policies should the U.S. change? In the midst of this, I heard a critical question that deserves some reflection.

It started with a friend pointing out that previous mass killers employed fertilizer and jetliners, so instead of blaming guns, blame godlessness. Another friend countered, "Anyone can be good and moral." So can we be good without God?

The question can only be asked after assuming answers to others. The first is, whose morals? To the shooter, homosexuals are wrong and killing them is right. To another, being gay is not wrong and killing them certainly is. To yet another, homosexual behavior is wrong but so is killing them. Three sets of moral values, each held sincerely.

We could discuss who gets to decide what is moral, but the more basic question is, where does morality come from? How is it, that humans are born with the capacity to determine what ought or ought not be? You have heard young children declare, "That's not fair!" C. S. Lewis writes that humans "are haunted by the idea of a sort of behavior they ought to practice."

157

Why does morality even matter? The answer is value. Those Orlando victims were human beings. Murder, theft, and dishonesty are wrong because they harm something valuable: people.   But if we are only a product of impersonal evolution, why do we have that intrinsic worth and how do we all happen to know it?

A rational conclusion from these questions is that a Moral Lawgiver exists outside of ourselves. God values humans and instills within us a sense of value and morality. To say otherwise is to deny objective morality, and accept that each should do what is right in his own eyes. Thinkers such as C. S. Lewis, Francis Collins, and Chuck Colson became former atheists because the God of the Bible was the only answer to the question of morality that made sense to them.

Sure, people can be moral without religion. Many non-Christians are decent, law-abiding citizens.   But the question points to a Sovereign God who values people even when we ignore our moral compass. With that kind of heavenly Father, it is no surprise that He would send Jesus to fulfill the law on our behalf (Rom. 8:3-4) and save us by grace through faith (Eph. 2:8). That is good news that sustains us when bad news and moral questions trouble us.

Stand Firm

July 13, 2016

It was my privilege to speak to one of America's top gun fighter pilots. I heard a podcast featuring a recent seminary graduate discussing his doctoral dissertation. A few weeks later, I interviewed the author of that paper, John Marselus, also a recipient of the USAF's Top Professional Fighter Pilot award.

Dr. Marselus' dissertation takes up a challenge for which he is uniquely qualified: find inspiration for Christian fathers from the experiences of a fighter pilot. Each chapter of his academic work has an epigraph recounting stories from his fighter pilot career, which illustrates his research and conclusions.

Perhaps the nose art on his A-10 Thunderbolt II in Desert Storm, "Ephesians 6:10-18," inspired his thesis. The verses describe the armor of God and the spiritual enemy we face. To summarize the application of his research, he writes, "Through taking up the roles and responsibilities of a husband and father in leading the family in priority, prayer, provision, protection, and preparation, a father and husband can experience the joy of marriage and the family as God created in the beginning in His grace and mercy. It is time for men to lead as they were designed to lead and as a flight lead would lead his formation into battle."

As we talked, he described his life work. "Ministry is my heart, and flying is my tent-making." Now as Director of Aviation at San Diego Christian College, he trains professional aviators, "but number one is their walk with the Lord." His own walk started young in life as he pondered the loss of his 19-year-old brother. At a Billy Graham meeting in Chicago, he took a stand for the truth of the gospel and placed his faith in Christ. That set the course for his life.

He spoke of his best "wing man," his wife, who is his inspiration. In his acceptance of the Top Gun Award in front of the "kings of the Air Force," he declared, "If I did anything right, all glory and honor goes to my Lord and Savior Jesus Christ who gives me breath of life and gifts to succeed. And I would not be the man I am without the love and support of my wife. This award goes to them." Those gathered rewarded his courage with sincere, not just polite, applause.

His message for you, dear Christian, is that when you have opportunity, stand for Christ and Truth with courage! "Be on the alert, stand firm in the faith, act like men, be strong. Let all that you do be done in love" (1 Cor. 16:13-14).

During our conversation, I never felt like I was talking to a stranger. I was speaking with a true American hero, a family man, a brother in Christ who knows what it means to lead with courage, speak truth to power, and stand firm in the faith. With God's help, we will do no less.

Neighbors

July 20, 2016

People like stories. Our lives are stories. We don't live in the abstract, so it makes sense that Jesus taught in stories. We call them parables, and Jesus intended them mostly for the responsive, not the resistant. He liked to say, "He who has ears to hear, let him hear."

Dr. Bernard Ramm taught seminary students that the golden rule of interpreting a parable is to determine the one central truth the parable is attempting to teach. We do not have the luxury of trying to pick apart a parable and make it an allegory since the single point is usually quite evident. An exception is when Jesus unpacks the parable for us, such as the story about planting seeds in different soils.

The central truth of the "Good Samaritan" story is about being a loving neighbor, which might be a better name for it. Jesus spun this tale after agreeing that love of God has implications for how you treat your neighbor. "Who is my neighbor?" the questioner responded, prompting the story telling.

Jesus told it better, but I would summarize the story (Luke 10:25-37) like this. Once upon a time robbers jumped a man, took everything he had, and beat him almost to death. Religious people passed by without helping. A man who came from a generally disrespected class of people went to great personal cost to help the victim. It was an unexpected plot twist in the little story.

161

The religious people (like the ones he was chatting with) were not loving, but the despised man was. Jesus challenged his hearers to note who treated the victim like a neighbor.

So let's apply the central truth principal. If you want to demonstrate your love of God, then love your neighbor. Your neighbor is someone who has a need that you can meet, and it may be costly. It may be an opportunity to explain to your neighbor that your love of God compels you to be of service.

Jesus wasn't trying to get to an "A-ha!" moment of intellectual enlightenment. He meant for his hearers to be affected. "Go and do the same," he challenged. Love the Lord your God and love your neighbor as yourself are the Great Commandments according to Jesus (Mat. 22:36-40).

My challenge is for you to consider who your neighbor is, as defined by Jesus. In modern parlance, "paying it forward" or "making a difference" is nice, but why do that? For the Christian, the answer is that it is an expression of faith affecting life. May your story be one that includes faith, love, and neighbors.

Identity

July 27, 2016

The cultural mood of the day is that people can and should create their own identity. Anyone who fails to recognize that identity, even unknowingly, is a bigot. It is bewildering.

I can't imagine being a young person growing up in such an environment. Back in my day, my fellow students were known by what they were good at, or what they enjoyed doing, like sports, music, or academics. Now it's not what you do, it's who you are that you must define and enforce.

Cameron McAllister, a young Christian speaker, recently spoke with students at the University of Massachusetts, Amherst. He was surprised by the questions students asked about meaning, purpose, and the nature of existence. He notes, "Our culture has replaced self-discovery with self-construction. Everybody is expected to create and manage his or her own identity. The pressure that this mindset creates is devastating."

In the movie "Catch Me," Leonardo DiCaprio played a teenager that became a criminal by fabricating false identities. For a while, he found success in passing as a pilot, an attorney, and a doctor. What became clear during the course of the movie is that his character was miserably tied up in knots trying to find elusive happiness in his next adopted identity. But no identity could change what he really was, an unhappy, heartless, and destructive young man.

God offers us a new identity in Christ. This identity is secondary to none, including profession and work, sexuality and gender, politics and worldview. Our identity in Christ is crafted by God and defines all others. We are part of something larger than ourselves, the Providential work of our Father who is accomplishing his purposes for creation. "It is no longer I who live, but Christ lives in me; and the life which I now live in the flesh I live by faith in the Son of God" (Gal. 3:20).

The New Testament is replete with details of our identity. Just in Romans 8 we find that we are alive to God, the dwelling place of His Spirit, and heirs with Christ. God leads us, turns all things to good for us, and calls us to join his purpose. We have no fear and no condemnation. Nothing separates us from God's great love. The Holy Spirit prays for us and Jesus intercedes for us. In short, we are children of God. To embrace this identity is to remove dividing distinctions, "for you are all one in Christ Jesus" (Gal. 3:28).

As Christians our identity is Jesus Christ. He said, "Blessed are you when people insult you…because of me," prescient and encouraging words since nowadays politically correct culture accepts almost any claimed identity but ours.

Money

August 3, 2016

I can't believe Jesus said THIS about money! OK, so I shouldn't try to write clickbait headlines for a living. But with the stock market up 20% in 2016 (which could change before this sees ink) and home values on the rise, money is talking. Jesus didn't hesitate to address topics as relevant today as 2000 years ago, including money. Here are five of his challenging comments on the subject.

1. "Calculate the cost." When I was in Haiti, a friend started building a mud-walled house without figuring the cost first. I reminded him of Jesus' story about counting the cost before starting a building. The point was about the cost of following Jesus. "None of you can be My disciple who does not give up all his own possessions," a very high cost. Authentic discipleship means submitting to Divine priorities as we steward God's possessions entrusted to us. (Luke 14:28-33)

2. "Render to Caesar." Which means pay your taxes. If you include all local, state, and federal taxes, Americans worked until May 10 this year just to render to Caesar. Americans pay more taxes than we spend on food, clothing, and housing combined. We could mount an argument about what is reasonable and elect leaders that lower our taxes, but defrauding the tax collector is not an option. (Mat. 22:15-22)

3. "Give to the poor." In the movie, "It's a Wonderful Life," Mr. Potter muttered to George Bailey that his

mortgages to the poor just created "a discontented, lazy rabble instead of a thrifty working class." That was not Jesus' view of the poor.   Sure, many suffer the consequences of poor choices, but finding appropriate ways to help is our calling as Christians. Jesus also said, "to the extent that you did it to one of the least, you did it to Me." (Mat. 6:1-4, 25:34-46)

4. "Do not worry about tomorrow." But we do, and yes, this is about money. Worry about financial matters, or any worry actually, leaves no room for faith. Jesus noted that our heavenly Father knows what we need, so we should "seek first His kingdom and His righteousness." We find freedom in letting tomorrow take care of itself. (Mat. 6:25-34)

5. "Not even when one has an abundance does his life consist of his possessions." In his story of the "Rich Fool," Jesus warned about prioritizing wealth.   Fortune magazine (Jan. 2016) reported that 44% of lottery winners were broke within five years, and nearly a third declared bankruptcy and ended up worse off than before they became rich. Be careful what you wish for. Be "rich toward God." (Luke 12:13-21)

Money is the object of the sin of greed. If you want to bend your heart Godward, invest in what matters to God. What you do with your money is what you do with your life. "You cannot serve God and money" – Jesus.

Last Chance

August 10, 2016

It was an awkward encounter. Anyone who carries the name and message of Christ will likely have similar stories. Since our worldview encompasses eternity, we are willing to take risks to change eternal outcomes.

Someone suggested I visit an elderly couple I didn't know. As I approached their front door one evening, I wondered how I would explain what I was doing there. The door opened just wide enough for me to see the wife's face, kind, but a bit apprehensive. I introduced myself and a couple of friends and mentioned our church. I said simply that a mutual friend asked us to stop by for a brief visit. "It's really not a good time," she said. A polite brush-off, which I respected. The door creaked, closing.

A faceless male voice called from the interior, "Who is it?" The creaking paused. "People from a church." "Well let them in!" The man was resting in a wheelchair, clearly not in good health, and perhaps hoping we could cheer him up a little.

Settling into the parlor, we tried polite conversation with little success. I ditched the trivialities. "Do you mind if I ask you a personal question about God?" He consented. "If you were to die and stand before God, and if He asked you, 'Why should I let you into my heaven?' what would you say?" He raised his eyebrows as he pondered. "Well, I've tried to live a good life. I haven't been able to go to church since I've been sick."

I began to explain some truth claims from the Bible, beginning with, "The gift of God is eternal life in Christ Jesus our Lord." Nothing wrong with trying to live a good life or attending church, but they are not enough. Sadly, despite our best efforts, we have all sinned and fallen short of God's moral standard, which is perfection. As a just God, He has said that "the wages of sin is death." Such is the human condition.

But God, not content to leave us to our fate, "demonstrates His own love toward us, in that while we were yet sinners, Christ died for us." Jesus takes our punishment and gives us the righteousness of God. This is where faith comes in. "By grace you have been saved through faith; and that not of yourselves, it is the gift of God." Faith receives what God gives. (Rom. 1:16-17, 5:8, 6:23, Eph. 2:8)

As I finished, he brightened considerably. "That all makes sense, I just haven't thought of it that way before. Yes, that's what I believe!" We thanked the gentle couple for their time and left.

A week later I received news that our host that evening died three days after our visit. I was stunned. Only God knows if he embraced faith in Jesus that night, but regardless, I was grateful for the privilege of offering what may have been his last chance to do so. You never know.

Mystic

August 17, 2016

A. W. Tozer was a pastor during the Roaring 20's, the Great Depression, WWII, Korean War and the 60's cultural upheavals. You might think what he had to say would be more relevant for those trying times than ours. Not so.

Some know Tozer from his writings on prayer. He is perhaps best known as author of The Pursuit of God, which Warren Wiersbe calls "one of the best devotional books ever written by an American pastor." That's remarkable, considering Tozer had no formal academic training. His lack of earned letters did not diminish his message about prayer and devotion to God whom he pursued with vigor.

He published this book just a few years after WWII as a collection of ten essays. Though a short book, it is not a quick read due to its intensity and depth. Consider his thoughts on Psa. 57:5, "Be Thou exalted, O God, above the heavens; let thy glory be above all the earth." He writes, "The cause of all our human miseries is a radical moral dislocation, an upset in our relation to God and to each other. (Mankind) destroyed the proper Creator-creature relation in which, unknown to him, his true happiness lay. Essentially, salvation is the restoration of a right relation between man and his Creator."

And Tozer thought there was a radical moral dislocation in 1948! People are still miserable and rather than turning to God, ignore Him who is the very source of true love and happiness. Culture today encourages people to invent god in their own image, to justify the very misery that Jesus can heal, and to blame those of us who have found the healing balm for our souls.

Tozer considered himself an evangelical mystic, an unusual label. He defines that as one "who has been brought by the gospel into intimate fellowship with the Godhead. He differs from the ordinary orthodox Christian only because he experiences his faith down in the depths of his sentient being. He exists in a world of spiritual reality. He is quietly, deeply aware of the presence of God." A mystic doesn't just have faith in his life, his life is shaped by his faith; he doesn't just know about God, he has an intimate fellowship with God.

If I understand the man, Tozer would not have you read his works on prayer for formulaic rituals, nor his devotionals for warm feelings. His challenge is to invite God into the depths of your being and become aware of His reality in the ordinary, joyful, and troubling moments of your daily existence. Then you will be not just a church-goer, but like Tozer, a mystic.

Olympians

August 24, 2016

The 2016 Olympics are complete. New records and newly awarded medals are in the books. During their moment in the spotlight, some of America's athletes explained their life's motivation.

Maya DiRado won four medals (two gold) at her first and only Olympics. A late bloomer at 24, she said it "is not my end purpose, to make the Olympic team. Jesus' love for me and all humanity is something that always helps me better love people around me. I think God cares about my soul and whether I'm bringing his love and mercy into the world. Can I be a loving, supportive teammate, and can I bless others around me in the same way God has been so generous with me?" She soon starts a new job in Atlanta as a business analyst.

David Boudia and Steele Johnson are platform divers. A repeat Olympian, Boudia said, "If I represent a good God, I need to be that visual representation of him all the time, not just when I feel like it." This, Johnson's first Olympics, was even sweeter since a severe diving accident almost sidelined him. "Yes I had that accident. But I still had the ability to dive, and I still had the passion for diving. God kept me alive and he is still giving me the ability to do what I do." After they won silver in synchronized diving, Boudia talked about the pressure to an NBC interviewer. "When my mind is on this, thinking I'm defined by this, then my mind goes crazy, but we both know our identity is in

Christ." Johnson added, "The fact that I was going into this event knowing that my identity is rooted in Christ and not this competition just gave me peace."

The "shot diva" Michelle Carter is the daughter of Michael Carter, an Olympic medalist and Super Bowl winner. She won shot put gold, tossing 9 pounds a distance of 68 feet. Raised in church, she gave her life to Christ at six years old. She began a Bible study with her Olympic teammates. "People notice how I am living out my faith. Even when no one is looking, the way I act is important because it is a reflection of how I walk with Christ." After Rio, she returns to life as a business owner.

These athletes echo Eric Liddell, the Scottish runner who medaled in the 1924 Olympics. He said, "We are all missionaries. Wherever we go we either bring people nearer to Christ or we repel them from Christ." God determines our appointed times and boundaries, whether athletes or not. God has given us "this treasure in earthen vessels, so that the surpassing greatness of the power will be of God and not from ourselves" (2 Cor. 4:6). Your life has its own platform to display this powerful treasure of greater value than gold, silver, or bronze.

Distractions

August 31, 2016

Every four years, Labor Day marks the beginning of the final push of a long political campaign cycle. The holiday that celebrates the accomplishments of the American worker is also when many start to pay attention to politics. I submit that work and politics can be distracting, but not how you might think.

Work is a distraction when it is simply a mundane means to money. You can view it either as how you are pressed to pass time, or better, how you are privileged to serve people. Every job at some level is about people. If not customers, clients, or consumers, at least it's about your family that benefits from your labor. But more than that, work is your opportunity to change the part of God's world that you touch. It is the place you influence people by your ethics, words, and performance. The Christian worker's calling is, "Do your work heartily, as for the Lord rather than for men...It is the Lord Christ whom you serve" (Col. 3:23-24). Work is not a distraction, it is your opportunity to live out your faith and values.

Politics is a distraction when it masquerades as the only solution. When the only tool you have is a hammer, every problem looks like a nail. Our vote is not our only tool, nor is every problem fixed by a vote. But it is easy to think so when most headlines scream about the politicians' latest problems, promises, and polls, and when well-meaning people explain that if we don't vote their way we are inviting disaster for the country, the church, or morality. Consider for a moment that God's response to the saints' pleading for a great spiritual awakening might look like this strange election. Where the world today is experiencing mass movement to Jesus, you don't find a church that is comfortable, free, and basking in a culture that embraces Biblical morality. For sure, vote your conscience, but don't let it distract you from praying, trusting God, and accepting His story for our history.

C. S. Lewis, in <u>Screwtape Letters</u>, has one demon writing to another that people "find it all but impossible to believe in the unfamiliar while the familiar is before their eyes. Keep pressing home on him the ordinariness of things. Do remember you are there to fuddle him." If work and politics are ordinary to us, then we are befuddled. But our heavenly Father has an extraordinary plan. Extraordinary things are not a distraction.

"Let us run with endurance the race that is set before us, fixing our eyes on Jesus, the author and perfecter of faith" (Heb. 12:1-2).

Football

It happened while I was in attendance at a football game of my alma mater, Auburn University. It was early in the season like now, not exactly cool fall temperatures. When the crowd roared as the team entered the field, I had an odd revelation. Football is a metaphor for the church.

In a football game, the audience focuses on the participants on the gridiron stage, and is prepared to celebrate if the team does well. If a worship service is people watching a stage performance, and congratulating the preacher with "Nice sermon!" at the end, it deserves a penalty flag. But when those on the stage lead the audience to be participants who focus on God, it is a worshipful celebration of a win that already happened. On a cross long ago, Jesus defeated sin and death for us. "Thanks be to God who gives us the victory through our Lord Jesus Christ" (1 Cor. 15:57). When you participate in God's grace by faith, the celebration is daily, not just on Sundays.

As I watched that game, I thought about how unexercised I had become since my high school football days. Another revelation. The players and coaches on the field did all the preparation, planning, and work while the lazy audience just paid to observe. Churches are dysfunctional when they view their pastor and other staff members as the hired guns who are supposed to do the ministry. The New Testament description of the church is that leaders equip every Christian to be a minister, ambassador, and worker for Christ. Applied to football, the coaches and players would be training the rest of us how to play our own scrimmage. "To each one is given the manifestation of the Spirit for the common good" (1 Cor. 12:7). What is given to us in love, grace, and kindness, we reinvest in the people around us.

Followers of Christ are teammates that help each other. I was privileged once to meet Coach Dan Reeves during the time of his success with the Atlanta Falcons. In a private moment, I asked if I could point out something that might be a blind spot. Maybe he was amused that a pastor thought he knew about football. I said, "I just wanted to make sure you know that when a call goes against your team, they focus the camera on your face, which makes lip-reading very easy." He chuckled and said he needed to keep that in mind. "Just trying to help," I said. "We who are many, are one body in Christ, and individually members one of another" (Rom. 12:5).

The church already has its victory in Jesus! What's left is for us to "run with patience the race that is set before us" (Heb. 12:1). The next time someone complains that you're too fond of football, explain that you enjoy pondering its metaphorical and ecclesiastical implications!

Visitors

September 14, 2016

I heard tires scrunching the gravel of my driveway as the car slowly crept toward where I stood in my yard. I noticed that the occupants were dressed very nicely for a Saturday morning. Then I realized I was being Visited.

I always welcome the opportunity for a robust conversation about religion. I appreciate that these folks were as gentle and polite as they were convinced and sincere. I was quite eager to make the case for who Jesus is. That is, by the way, how you can tell historical Christianity from its modern variations.

From the outset of John's gospel, Jesus is God. Not just a son of God, but God the Son. The Word was with God in the beginning, and "the Word was God." All things, even life itself, came into being through the Word. This Word became flesh, so no doubt this Word is Jesus (John 1). So, if the Creator is God, then Jesus is. To supply the indefinite article as in, the Word was "a" god, misunderstands the grammar of Koine Greek. Worse, it implies polytheism, quite foreign to historic Christianity. Not to mention that John's context clearly describes the existence and activity of God. The word "Trinity" does not have to occur in the Bible for it to provide systematic evidence for one God in Three Persons.

Did Jesus claim to be God? In one instance, Jesus mentioned Abraham (who lived over a thousand years prior), which his hearers didn't appreciate. "You are not yet fifty years old, and have you seen Abraham?" they retorted. Jesus said, "Before Abraham was born, I am" (John 8:58). How could Jesus have existed that long ago? And why didn't he say, "I was" or just "Abraham and I are old friends!" To Moses at his burning bush, God revealed his name, I AM. I wonder if Jesus' hearers looked around to see if there was another burning bush, because He just called himself by that Name.

Do the Hebrew Scriptures anticipate the Messiah would be a God-man? The prophet Isaiah describes a virgin-born child who would be called "Eternal Father" and nothing less than "Mighty God" (Isa. 9:6). Daniel describes the "Son of Man" with godly dominion over an eternal kingdom, a title Jesus applied to himself (Dan. 7:13-14).

You can deny that Jesus is God the Son, but to do so you must explain away much evidence in the Bible. The reason it exists is so you can know God and receive eternal life by faith in Christ Jesus.

After my visitors left, I realized my mistake. I spent too much effort on the debate and not enough offering Jesus' saving grace. I won't make that same mistake with you, dear reader. I invite you to believe the Truth, and live!

Regret

September 21, 2016

As he told his story, I could hear pain, if not see it in his eyes. The story was not unlike mine and yours, since we all would like a redo on events of the past. But even though we cannot change the past, we can deal with it in the present and future.

His story was a case of "what-if." As a young man, his father invited him on a business-related road trip that would involve long hours driving a vehicle. He felt like his reason for not going was trivial, especially given the consequences. There was a horrible accident. His father may have fallen asleep at the wheel. We'll never know for sure. "What if I had gone with him?" Even if he had, the outcome could have been worse, not better. His mother may have been burying a son also, not just a husband. His regret was a cancer of the soul.

Regret over missed opportunities, wrong choices, and unfortunate reactions can harangue a person with troubling voices. "That was a stupid thing to do. I'm stupid." "I failed, so I'm worthless." "I'm unlovable and I'll never forgive myself." The term "skeletons in the closet" implies they're always there, ready to rattle their bones and haunt you. It doesn't have to be that way.

Christian truth is for life today, not just eternity. You see that in Jesus' many ordinary encounters with hurting people. If there was ever a man to have regret, it would be Jesus' disciple Peter. He followed Jesus for years,

179

watching him heal, teach, and prophecy. He had ample reason to love and trust Jesus. Then came that dark night when fear and self-preservation overcame that love and trust. Peter thrice denied even knowing Jesus. Remorse. Shame. Regret.

Jesus understands the human condition. He knew Peter loved him and meant no harm. So there on the beach, after a breakfast of fish and bread cooked over charcoal, Jesus asked Peter three times if he loved him. Each time Peter responded "yes," Jesus gave him an assignment showing he was forgiven, loved, and needed. Jesus wanted no haunting skeletons in Peter's closet. (John 21)

Nor does he want any in yours. Faith in Jesus means accepting that only He can restore that image of God in you that is marred by the human experience. His forgiveness empowers you to redeem the past by learning from its mistakes, accepting its consequences, and making it right if you can. Jesus loves you and wants you in his grand enterprise of spreading His love to the rest of the hurting world. "If we live, we live for the Lord" (Rom. 14:8). You can do that much better without carrying around the weight of un-healed regret.

History Lesson

September 28, 2016

Polls aren't just for politics. The recent Pew Religious Landscape Survey found some interesting trends about Christianity in America. A glance back in history can help us make sense of it.

The Survey found a decline in the number of Americans that identify as Christian, and an increase in the "nones" (people with no religion). The secular media concluded that Christianity in America is dying. But on closer examination we find that regular church attenders remained constant, and the number of evangelicals increased. So what's happening? It seems that as the culture becomes increasingly secular, nominal (name-only) Christians are giving up the pretense.

A history lesson would help here. The colonial church in America was stagnant in the early 1700's. Church membership was in decline, likely due to scandals such as the infamous witch trials. To stem the loss, churchmen developed a dubious plan to offer "halfway" membership for those assenting to church teachings, but not willing to embrace Jesus and "convert."

Into this awkward mix of nominal Christianity and skeptical culture Jonathan Edwards was born. His diary reveals that as a Yale student in 1720, a Bible passage moved him to enthusiastically convert to Christianity. There, he read about unbelief and mercy, Christ Jesus the patient Savior of sinners, and eternal life. "Now to the King eternal, immortal, invisible, the only God, be honor and glory" expressed the rapture of his soul! (1 Tim. 1:17)

Later as a pastor, he preached about the Savior and began to witness remarkable and extraordinary events leading to mass conversions. The Great Awakening continued for 10 years. Its vast outdoor meetings of up to 20,000 souls foreshadowed deserted taverns, packed churches, and changed communities.

This history and the afore-mentioned survey reveal the difference between "church-ianity" and Christianity; between religious affiliation and saving faith in Jesus Christ. Whether half-members, nominal Christians, or nones, people need a relationship with the Savior who is the same yesterday and today and forever. (Heb. 13:8). The church has no option or need to compromise truth per the demands of culture. Unpopular truth is still true.

The church today is strong among convictional Christians even as it is jettisoned by the "nones." There is a winnowing, you might say. A clarifying moment for all parties. Perhaps God will bring about another Awakening. If so, we won't need a Pew Survey to tell us He did.

Will to Live

October 5, 2016

Every day you wake up is a day you have chosen to live. Evidence suggests that the human mind and its will to live can shorten or lengthen life. Let me share about two people I once knew.

As a hospice chaplain I received the case of a middle-aged woman with brain cancer. She knew she was dying, which only made her more thankful for each day of life. She expressed a firm faith in Christ, and was assured of her eternity. She was tenacious, and had already out-lived the expectations of doctors.

Yet the day came when she became unresponsive. Lying in her own bed at home, she continued to live unassisted by medical devices. Her family waited. During my visits I talked to her and prayed with her since it is possible that an unresponsive person can still understand. One day I shared with her it is OK to let go, that by faith she knew she was not of this world. Her future held more promise than her present. The next day she was gone. Coincidence or choice?

Haiti was a cash economy when I lived there. I was responsible for certain purchases in Port au Prince for my organization, which required traveling with sums of money that would stagger the typical $5 per day worker. The drive from the Artibonite Valley was about 4 hours, which required a very early departure and a grueling day of travel.

The day of one such trip, I tossed my backpack with the cash into the jeep. In those pre-dawn hours not a soul stirred in our village. I stopped to pick up a colleague, and stepped to his door, a mere 20 feet away. I heard a sound and looked back at the vehicle, seeing nothing in the darkness. I soon discovered that the backpack was gone.

The village knew who did it. In a few days, before the wheels of justice could turn, the young man's family rushed him to the hospital. He later died. The Harvard-trained medical director told me that he could identify no physical cause of death. He speculated that the young man was so shocked and afraid by the magnitude of his theft that he willed himself to die.

The Christian faith offers a reason to live, and paradoxically requires choosing to die. Jesus said, "Whoever wishes to save his life will lose it, but whoever loses his life for My sake and the gospel's will save it" (Mark 8:35). Paul understood it this way: "I have been crucified with Christ; and it is no longer I who live, but Christ lives in me" (Gal. 2:20). Let your will to live be enriched with the joy, hope, and peace of sharing in the life of Christ.

The Ark

October 12, 2016

Noah was the Rodney Dangerfield of his day. He still doesn't get much respect. Even so, the tale of an ark, a flood, and a heroic man are no joke. In this epic story we find a reflection of our times, and truths for life.

Earlier this year, the Ark Encounter opened in Williamstown, Kentucky. Billed as "a life-sized Noah's Ark," the 510 ft long boat is a museum dedicated to the plausibility of the Genesis account. Even with Harvard-educated biologist Dr. Nathaniel Jeanson as advisor, Ken Ham's project to demonstrate the plausibility of the creation story has (not surprisingly) earned little respect from those who believe in evolution. But allow me to step away from this modern controversy to focus on the lessons from the life and times of Noah.

Things seemed to be going well when "the sons of God saw that the daughters of men were beautiful, and they took wives." But the romance didn't last. In time, "the Lord saw that the wickedness of man was great on the earth" (Gen. 6). If wickedness is man calling good what God says is evil, and man calling evil what God says is good, then surely we, too, live in perverted and wicked times.

But we don't have to fall into self-destructive beliefs and behaviors according to Jesus' confidant Peter. He observed that if God knew how to preserve Noah even while not sparing the ancient world from the flood, then surely "the Lord knows how to rescue the godly from temptation" (2 Pet. 2:4-9). Do you trust him to do that for you? If you fear of losing it, of giving in, remember Noah. God called him to act contrary to the culture of unbelief, and preserved him through it.

Noah was spared because of his righteousness, which we know comes by faith (Heb. 11:7). The prophet Ezekiel quoted God saying that even a righteous man like Noah couldn't help "if a country sins against Me by committing unfaithfulness." The good news is that God knows the believers in a nation even if He decides to "stretch out My hand against it" (Eze. 14:13-14).

Jesus spoke of Noah as real, not a myth. "Just as it was in the days of Noah" describes people oblivious about God, morality, and the promised end times. "It will be just the same on the day that the Son of Man is revealed" (Luke 17:30). But just as the ark brought Noah to safety, the resurrected Jesus Christ at the right hand of God can "bring us to God" (1 Pet. 3:18-20).

Visit the Ark Encounter if you're interested in the debate about Creation vs. Evolution, truth vs. myth, and how many animals can fit in a ship. Until then, you have your own encounter when you embrace the lessons of God's ark and his servant Noah.

Authenticity

October 19, 2016

Everyone lives out a philosophy or religion whether aware of it or not. It is axiomatic that if you follow a path, you think it is the right one. But just because it is right for you does not necessarily mean that it is "Christian." Believers and non-believers alike can mistake sincerity or appearances for authentic faith.

In another time, another place, I knew of a church that was attacked like a wolf in sheep's clothing. A humble but well-to-do businessman joined them, but didn't really seek attention. He was encouraging, supportive, and generous. He knew the language of the Christian faith. He let it be known that he was an investment manager. Little by little the details emerged about his portfolio returning 25% or more annually with no risk. Soon he was signing up new customers at church. It was a pyramid scheme. He was eventually arrested and convicted. Most of his victims lost everything they invested, some their life savings. He appeared sincere, but was not authentic.

The Bible addresses authenticity thoroughly. The Lord understands the human tendency to fake it, and most posers aren't as blatant as the criminal in my story. A Hebrew prophet spoke to people who were quite religious, but had forsaken the Lord. "I delight in loyalty rather than sacrifice, and in the knowledge of God rather than burnt offerings" (Hos. 6:6).

187

Jesus said, "Not everyone who says to Me, 'Lord, Lord,' will enter the kingdom of heaven" (Mat. 7:21). He knew people would claim his name without submitting to the Father's will. He told parables about seeds that sprout and appear healthy until challenged, and weeds growing amidst the wheat. Is this not about authenticity? He spoke about a small gate and a narrow way "and there are few who find it," which can be alarming (Mat. 7:13-14).

John's first epistle has multiple tests of authentic faith. Has his grace moved you to admit sin, abide in Him, and love one another in deed and truth? If you have exchanged your life for His, you practice righteousness, confess the Son, and know the Spirit of God. Once I led a dialogue on this, and a venerable old saint asked, "Are we to test each other?" "No. We examine ourselves," I countered.

Amidst these clarifying challenges, John writes, "These things I have written to you who believe in the name of the Son of God, so that you may know that you have eternal life" (1 Jn. 5:13). We do not have to stumble through life wondering. We can know for certain that we have authentic faith. That's good news!

Halloween

October 26, 2016

Halloween, or "holy evening," for most is a masquerade party with candy as a reward, harmless unless you're concerned about the effect of sugar on the human body. For some, it is a day of celebrating a certain other-world spirituality. Myths and fables about not-so-holy ghosts and goblins, witches and black cats, jack-o'-lanterns and skeletons all hint at a fixation on death and evil in this world. No wonder churches prefer a fall harvest festival or Reformation Day event.

A witch doctor in Haiti once told me that October 31 is the day in which the veil between this life and the next is the thinnest. Thinking it culturally instructive to see a ceremony to conjure up a spirit, I considered attending a night festival in the nearby village of Liancourt on that date. But older, wiser folks convinced me I had no business there. Voodoo practitioners foster an aura of fear and mystery to build a marketable practice of folk justice and healing. The Christian worldview that acknowledges personal evil must allow the possibility that such occultic activities are not harmless.

The Bible describes an act of necromancy, or calling up the dead. It is a story easy to retell, but hard to explain. Israel's King Saul knew that God had forbade his people to use divination, witchcraft, sorcery, and necromancy, and had applied that law during his reign. Yet after he had turned away from God, and found that God would not

189

answer his prayers for courage and wisdom in the face of the Philistine army, he decided to violate that command.

Saul disguised himself, and sought a medium, "the witch of En-dor." She hesitated, mentioning the prohibition. He persisted, wanting her to bring up the dead prophet Samuel. The apparition frightened the woman conjurer, and said that Saul and his sons were to die in battle the next day. Saul looked for an answer in the wrong place.

If occult activities are harmless, why would God prohibit them? To seek that kind of spiritual encounter is to acknowledge a spiritual power other than God, which is idolatrous. The Bible explains that spiritual evil does exist with the purpose to steal, kill, and destroy. We are to resist, not embrace it.

God wants us to seek Him. "Resist the devil and he will flee from you. Draw near to God and He will draw near to you" (Jas. 4:7-8). God has revealed Himself to be near us and for us, so "let us draw near with confidence to the throne of grace, so that we may receive mercy and find grace to help in time of need" (Heb. 4:16). By grace through faith in Christ it is we that are holy (i.e. "saints" 1 Cor. 1:2), not a date on a calendar.

Personal, Not Private

November 2, 2016

You have heard politicians say they are personally opposed to a policy, "But I don't want to impose my beliefs on others." That's intended to sound noble, even humble. It can also mean, "I have convictions but they don't matter." Which doesn't sound like convictions at all. Seems more like political calculation than leadership. Shouldn't personal convictions affect your public life?

Don't worry. This isn't about politics, it's really about all of us. The answer to the question is yes, particularly for a Christian. Faith is personal, but not meant to be private.

It is personal because it is your individual faith in a God who has revealed Himself, experienced in a community that identifies with Jesus Christ. Such faith doesn't come pre-packaged with a baby nor is it available in bulk by joining a group of believers. Hopefully those believers follow Jesus in such a way that you want to receive his grace, personally.

Jesus explained to Nicodemus that he must be born again in order to enter the kingdom of God (John 3:3). Peter wrote that Jesus "caused us to be born again to a living hope through the resurrection of Jesus Christ from the dead" (1 Pet. 1:3). The phrase "born again" isn't a certain type of Christian; it is normative for all who claim His name and describes something quite personal and individual.

191

In his book <u>Against the Flow</u>, Dr. John Lennox notes the challenge of living a personal faith in public. "Strong currents of pluralism and secularism in contemporary Western society, reinforced by a paralyzing political correctness, increasingly push expression of faith in God to the margins." Yet Jesus called us to be salt and light, metaphors of engaging culture in a public way. "Let your light shine before men in such a way that they may see your good works, and glorify your Father," Jesus said (Mat. 5:16).

Peter heard Jesus say, "Everyone who confesses Me before men, I will also confess him before My Father" (Mat. 10:32). But he blew it when he denied Jesus quite publicly. Three times. Fortunately Jesus forgave and restored him after the Resurrection when he affirmed his faith three times publicly. Later when arrested for proclaiming Jesus, Peter courageously declared, "We must obey God rather than men!" (Acts 5:29). His disregard for the consequences is like "d--- the torpedoes, full steam ahead!" (regards to Admiral Farragut!).

To take a stand for the Way, Truth, and Life will increasingly call for resolve, and has already caused consequences for some. No this isn't about politics, but join me in praying for leaders, judges, and laws that do not infringe on our freedom to express our personal faith publicly.

Hip Hop

November 9, 2016

Our cities are in trouble. America's pathologies are concentrated in its urban centers, evidenced by murder and mayhem, heartbreak and hopelessness, crime and corruption. Politicians don't seem to be changing anything but I recently heard something that just might.

I was at a conference to hear how Christians can respond to our changing culture. But never in a million years did I expect to hear rap music! Perhaps it is tragically too easy for some of us to look away from a segment of culture that seems like a lost cause.

Emanuel Lambert, from Philadelphia, explained that rap music and the hip hop subculture express the deep frustrations of the inner city. He notes that this culture has many painful and tragic questions that too often become sad headlines and crime statistics. Voicing the questions can build a bridge of understanding, across which can travel some truthful answers that can set a life on a new trajectory.

Mr. Lambert is a rap artist known as "DA' T.R.U.T.H." He is a committed Christian with 20 years in the music industry as an award-winning artist. He is well-connected in the hip hop community and recently formed the entertainment company NXT Sound. He also knows Ravi Zacharias, a Christian apologist and evangelist, and invited the 70-year-old native of India to speak on his recent album, "It's Complicated."

In the selection "Religion," the rapper poses the question, *Are all religions equal, can we even know?* in the voice of the 'hood.   In rhythmic cadence he asks, *Did I blindly believe when I got a Bible to read? Then I got down on my knees as the one way to God. Dropped down to plead, a total waist of my time? Is his name a lie, or is his name Allah? Is it really important, the right name or not?*

Then as part of the song track, Dr. Zacharias answers, *Pantheism doesn't teach the same thing as theism. Monotheistic beliefs are not all the same.   What Islam believes about Allah and what the Christian believes about the Triune God are two different things.   All religions, at best, are superficially similar, but they are fundamentally different.   The song responds with, How many paths to God? If it's one I'm taking my steps. We are all on a journey together, and I know that there's a God out there that can make my eternity better.*

The next time your stopped car vibrates at a red light, the culprit could be truth. Chanted Loudly! A small price to pay if it changes lives.   Mr. Lambert is convening a meeting soon to introduce other artists to Dr. Zacharias. If that begins to transform the hip hop community with truthful answers, America will be a better place, a reason to hope!

Names

November 16, 2016

An off-duty policeman in the city was enjoying his day off. He walked down to the corner coffee shop for a wakeup brew. He glanced around as he was about to enter, and suddenly sprinted to the curb to grab a blind man about to step into traffic. "Thief!" the blind man screamed as he swatted the policeman with his cane, misunderstanding what just happened. Nursing his bruised pride, the hero said he would do it again.

I recently heard Os Guinness observe that culture has "re-branders." The term describes an effort to redefine something as other (thief) than intended (hero). Professor Michael Rectenwald at NYU knows about this. His anonymous blog criticized the safe spaces and trigger warnings that coddle students and their social justice ideas. The administration relieved him of his classroom duties because what he called academic freedom, they called incivility. I call it political correctness.

It's anachronistic to label what happened in ancient Babylon as P.C., but it fits. Four young Hebrew men with names that reminded them of their God, were exiled to a foreign land and renamed to obscure their past allegiances. They were re-branded. Yet Daniel and his fellow believers continued to live out their faith in the one true God even when facing the lion's den and the fiery furnace. They went along until their consciences stopped them.   Forced uniformity has its limits.   Remember Orwell's <u>1984</u>?

Lurking about is a movement to re-brand religious freedom as bigotry, making the First Amendment a sword instead of a shield.   Martin Castro reported for the U.S. Commission on Civil Rights that efforts to protect religious freedom is really a cover for discrimination, and must be curbed.   Is it far-fetched to consider this a proto-threat that could lead to the prohibition Peter faced, "Do not speak in name of Jesus" (Acts 4:18)?

The passive Christian response is to syncretize our faith with whatever the culture embraces. Responding to the recent Jen Hatmaker controversy, Rosaria Butterfield wrote, "Sin and Christ cannot abide together, for the cross never makes itself an ally with the sin it must crush, because Christ took our sin upon himself and paid the ransom for its dreadful cost!" Will we rename what God says is sin to blend with a culture that desperately needs redeeming?

Christians bear the Name of the One who loves all sinners and offers the gift of abundant life. Even if P.C., re-branders, and government reports hit us with their canes, we will still reach out in love, again and again. People can embrace or deny Truth, but they can't change it. May the Name of our Lord Jesus be glorified in you, and you in Him, according to the grace of our God (1 Thes. 1:12).

Thanksgiving 2016

November 23, 2016

We are a nation divided. Voter sentiment in the national election is so close to 50-50 that polls cannot predict the outcome. Both sides ask the question, "How can they even conceive of voting for that person?" Americans are frustrated over sharply different philosophies of government. Our most notable disagreement in history resulted in the horrific Civil War. Our response now can be well-informed by what Abraham Lincoln did then.

Writing to various presidents for 15 years, Sara Hale lobbied for a national Thanksgiving observance on a fixed date. Lincoln agreed with her. On October 3, 1863, 74 years after George Washington's first thanksgiving proclamation, and juxtaposed with the Battle of Chickamauga and its 33,000 casualties just two weeks prior, Lincoln called for a national day of Thanksgiving on the last Thursday in November (later changed to fourth Thursday).

His 500-word proclamation still rings true. Lamenting that Americans are prone to forget the source of our blessings, he listed them beginning with "fruitful fields and healthful skies." Despite the War, "peace has been preserved with all nations." The War had not "arrested the plough, the shuttle or the ship." He noted increased development and population, the productivity of mines and industry, and the growth of the nation. "No human counsel hath devised nor hath any mortal hand worked out these great things. They are the gracious gifts of the Most High God."

Lincoln also urged "humble penitence for our national perverseness and disobedience" and petitions for "all those who have become widows, orphans, mourners or sufferers in the lamentable civil strife." He closed with a call to pray for "the Almighty Hand to heal the wounds of the nation and to restore it as soon as may be consistent with the Divine purposes to the full enjoyment of peace, harmony, tranquility and union."

Americans are still blessed for what we have, and for evil things that were not but might have been. We need forgiveness for the perversity of our times, and compassion for the defenseless and less fortunate among us. But above all thanksgiving implies a source, and Lincoln rightly understood that we thank the Most High God and submit to His purposes for our nation.

Our current strife has many faces. Riots in the streets. Pejoratives on our tongues. Anger on social media. It doesn't have to be that way. When we see the "Imago Dei" in one another, we cannot harbor such acrimony. If Lincoln could find reason to be thankful, surely we can. "Let them give thanks to the Lord for His lovingkindness, and for His wonders to the sons of men! For He has satisfied the thirsty soul, and the hungry soul He has filled with what is good" (Psa. 107:8-9).

Post-Truth

November 20, 2016

Selecting the word of the year is a self-assigned role of the Oxford University Press. The word for 2016 is "post-truth," meaning "objective facts are less influential in shaping public opinion than appeals to emotion and personal belief."

In other words, truth is less important than how you feel about it. They cite the Brexit vote and the U. S. election as evidence, which might be a bit ideological, implying that facts were ignored.

The raw campaign rhetoric makes me disinclined to stand for office since, for example, I shoo my cat off the kitchen table. My opponent could claim I hate furry pets and should be locked up as an animal molester! That's about as absurd as the post-truth spin from the 2016 campaigns.

The first time I noticed post-truth was Dan Rather's blunder that led to his resignation from CBS in 2004. While acknowledging the false evidence behind his story about George Bush's National Guard record, he insisted, "That didn't change the truth of what we reported." Unproven belief became truth.

Response to science can be post-truth. Medicine tells us that a fetus is alive, genetically independent, and human, yet only her mother is a person with inalienable rights to life. Cosmogony offers interesting hypotheses for the origins of the universe, yet the evidence of an intelligent First Source must not be considered.

Apparently a culture disconnected from truth is intolerant, assumes evil motives, and prefers ad hominem over constructive disagreement. It claims to be pluralistic, embracing all truths and voices. Yet without realizing the illogic, it excludes those who know contradictory claims can't all be true. If disagreement means harm and requires safe spaces, we are raising a crippled generation unable to think critically. For our own good, the Bible urges us not to mistake the truth of God for a lie (Rom. 1:25).

Vince Vitale, Director of the Zacharias Institute, observed that since Jesus is the truth (John 14:6) and God is love (1 Jn. 4:8), then truth is love. As such, one implication is that withholding truth to avoid a disagreement is just as unloving as a caustic argument. Disagreements can be loving and respectful. "Do not let kindness and truth leave you...write them on the tablet of your heart" (Prov. 3:3).

The truth matters about our world, our country, and ourselves. You can spin, twist, bend, and bury the truth, which is what happened to Jesus. Yet the truth lives to set you free from whatever binds you from the life and eternity God has planned for you. He has revealed truth in creation, in the Bible, and in our Savior, Jesus Christ. We who embrace faith in the only One who makes sense of this world can never be post-truth.

Cuba

December 7, 2016

Speaking to Christianity Today, after his escape from Cuba in 2012, Pastor Carlos Lamelas described a life of constant surveillance, attempts at black market entrapment, assaults and beatings, false accusations and imprisonment. Yet world leaders memorialize Fidel Castro as a successful socialist rather than a tyrant. He may be dead, but his intolerance of religious freedom in Cuba lives.

America's founders envisioned a government that answered to the people, who answer to God. Castro wanted the people to answer to him only. He founded an atheistic state, typical of 20th century communism. What it purports to offer comes at the price of freedom, a point today's socialists might consider.

After the fall of the USSR, Cuba ended its official policy of atheism. Churches grew as people looked for answers and found Christ. Since new church buildings are not permitted, a government official suggested home meetings. Castro accepted overtures from the Catholic Church. But the detente turned back in 2015, with agents citing a new law to justify repression of churches.

Between 2014 and 2015, the number of religious freedom violations increased tenfold to 2300 cases according to Christian Solidarity Worldwide. In the first half of 2016, authorities targeted 1600 churches including demolition and confiscation of property, and imprisonment of church leaders. Cuba still monitors and controls most aspects of religious life. "Serious religious freedom violations continue in Cuba, despite improvements for government-approved religious groups," according to the U.S. Commission on Religious Freedom (2015).

Despite the oppression, the church in Cuba is growing rapidly. Christians still meet in homes and historic church buildings. When a church outgrows a home, it multiplies to other homes. CBN reports that in the last 20 years, Cubans started more than 16,000 churches. The Baptists helped reinvigorate a failing seminary, which in 2008 graduated 150 pastors from an enrollment of 650. The boot-heel of government so far has not been efficient in stamping out faith, love, and hope.

The church in Cuba, Iran, and China have something in common: Persecution and sustained growth. History indicates that these go hand-in-hand. Jesus wanted his followers to be prepared for this. "If they persecuted Me, they will also persecute you" (John 15:20). Peter wrote, "Do not be surprised at the fiery ordeal among you, which comes upon you for your testing" (1 Pet. 4:12).

With travel restrictions lifted, American Christians are moving quickly to support our Cuban family. Franklin Graham has issued a call to purchase Bibles for distribution in Cuba. We can learn from those who "have been distressed by various trials so that the proof of your faith...may be found to result in praise, glory, and honor at the revelation of Jesus Christ" (1 Pet. 1:6-7). Now that he has met his Maker, perhaps Castro has learned something too, that his tyranny of the church has failed.

202

Evangelicals

December 14, 2016

Voting evangelicals are quite interesting to political scientists. One reason is that evangelicals comprise 25 to 35 percent of American adults. Just who are these evangelicals?

Christians are considered evangelical in three ways: how we self-identify, what church we attend, and what we believe. Anyone can claim the label, and no definitive list of evangelical churches exists, so the most precise way to determine an evangelical is by beliefs.

The National Association of Evangelicals and Lifeway Research developed a method to measure evangelical beliefs using four statements. If you strongly agree with these statements, they consider you an evangelical. Here they are:

1. The Bible is the highest authority for what I believe. A friend once challenged me, "Since men wrote it, how could it be the word of God?" Smart folks have written entire books on this. I'll just offer that the Bible has a consistent narrative that spans thousands of years, including prophecies fulfilled. It offers a worldview that makes sense of the world as we experience it. Risking a circular argument, I'll add that it claims to reveal what God wants us to know.

2. It is very important for me personally to encourage non-Christians to trust Jesus Christ as their Savior. One of Jesus' last utterances in the flesh was, "Make disciples

of all the nations, baptizing them in the name of the Father and the Son and the Holy Spirit" (Mat. 28:19). Followers do what the leader says.

3.   Jesus Christ's death on the cross is the only sacrifice that could remove the penalty of my sin. The Hebrew prophet foretold a suffering servant who would be crushed for our iniquities (Isa. 53:5). Peter confirmed that servant was Jesus. "Christ died for sins once for all, the just for the unjust, so that He might bring us to God" (1 Pet. 3:18).

4. Only those who trust in Jesus Christ alone as their Savior receive God's free gift of eternal salvation. Defending his preaching about Jesus, Peter said, "there is no other name under heaven that has been given among men by which we must be saved" (Acts 4:12). It is a free gift, received by faith (Eph. 2:8).

Exit polls in 2016 indicate that evangelicals do not agree on politics. But we do agree that in Christ "There is neither Jew nor Greek, slave nor free, male, nor female" (Gal. 3:28). And no democrat or republican. Our unity is not in our politics, but this: When we consider what Jesus alone has done for us as described in the Bible, it lifts our hearts heavenward, and compels us to share that good news with anyone who will listen. Such is the life and belief of an evangelical.

Christmas Hero

December 21, 2016

Talking with Johnny Carson in 1987 about "It's a Wonderful Life," Jimmy Stewart said, "It's amazing that it's become such a Christmas picture." It should be no surprise since the movie ends in a heart-warming Christmas scene, and a plot theme is full of the Christmas message.

Director Frank Capra's movie portrays the humble life of George Bailey. Despite his wanderlust of anchor chains, plane motors, train whistles, and his idealistic plans of changing the world, he stayed home. His father died and left the responsibility for the town building and loan business to George. In his work, he was admired and respected as he protected the town from the miserly Henry Potter.

George Bailey was a hero. He did not know what he meant to his family and friends until he saw what Bedford Falls might be like had he never been born. How fitting that they honored their hero at Christmas.

We are attracted to heroes, especially real ones. Just this month two policemen in Americus Georgia sacrificed their lives protecting their community from a lifelong, violent criminal. It became a national story, with condolences pouring in from around the country. May God strengthen these hero families in their time of grief and lifelong loss.

To truly understand the Christmas story, you must see the world from God's perspective. He sees people walking in darkness, living in a dark land, who need light. He sees people going astray like sheep, turning to our own way, who need a shepherd. (Isa. 9, 53)

Into such a world a child was born, and "His name will be called Wonderful Counselor, Mighty God, Eternal Father, Prince of Peace" (Isa. 9:6). This child was from above, as "He was in the beginning with God" (John 1:2). He was also from below, as his mother Mary "wrapped Him in cloths, and laid Him in a manger" (Luke 2:7). He is God in the flesh, God with us, the God who saves.

Jesus is our hero. His mission on earth was to be light, to be a shepherd, to be the way back to our Creator. What would our lives be like if he had never been born, never completed his mission? Paul tells us, "If Christ has not been raised, your faith is worthless; you are still in your sins" (1 Cor. 15:17). I shudder to think what the world would be without the love of God manifest to us in Christ's birth, life, death and resurrection.

Linus in "A Charlie Brown Christmas" explains the true meaning of Christmas. "I bring you good tidings of great joy, which shall be to all people. For unto you is born this day in the city of David a Savior, which is Christ the Lord" (Luke 2:10-11, KJV). Our Christmas hero.

2016 In Review

December 28, 2016

Pondering the events of the past year means revisiting the good, bad, and ugly. Before I attempt to make sense of it, let's review the history.

Sports are a good place to start. The Chicago Cubs clinched their first World Series title in 108 years. The Atlanta Braves finished the season well, leaving us optimistic about the first season in SunTrust Park. The U.S. won the most Olympic medals.

In politics, Donald Trump outpolled Hillary Clinton to become President-Elect. The Presidents of Brazil and South Korea were impeached, but the President of Turkey remained after an attempted coup. Teresa May became Prime Minister of the UK after the Brexit vote. Taiwan's first female president Tsai Ing-wen famously called Mr. Trump.

Now for the bad. Targeting police became a thing in 2016. At least 64 officers were killed, including four Dallas officers ambushed while protecting those protesting against them.

Hurricane Matthew killed hundreds and left thousands homeless in Haiti. Wildfires raged in Appalachia and California. Drought contributed to the damage and deaths as Gatlinburg burned. Louisiana and West Virginia flooded. Earthquakes hit Ecuador, New Zealand, and Italy, killing hundreds. The Zika virus reared its ugly head.

The "axis of evil" stirred the pot. North Korea became a nuclear power, and Iran rushed to join the club. Iran captured ten U.S. sailors and their boats, and is allied with Russia in Syria. The U.S. paid $400M to Iran.

The U.S. revealed ISIS killed 19,000 civilians since its beginning. Terrorists struck an Orlando club, Manhattan's Chelsea district, a Minnesota mall, and the Ohio State campus. Brussels, Paris, Istanbul, Cairo, and Berlin were attacked. Over 4000 died attempting to cross the Mediterranean Sea to escape terrorism in North Africa and the Middle East.

God has already accounted for the good and bad that happen. Theologians call this Providence, which is God's activity to direct a fallen creation to accomplish His divine purpose. Indeed, His purpose is personal. Remember the story of Esther, who lived for "such a time as this"? He knows the world you live in, having determined your appointed times and the boundaries of your habitation, that you would seek Him. When things happen that make you yearn for the good, the loving, and the merciful, they point to something outside yourself. Paul concluded that yearning is to know Christ and the power of his resurrection. (Esth. 4:14, Acts 17:26, Phil. 3:10)

With the Christmas story of peace and goodwill fresh on our hearts, we rest assured that God is unsurprised and undaunted. Nothing can separate us from the love of God, especially not the events now inscribed in the history book of 2016.

Scripture References

1 Cor. 1:18, 154
1 Cor. 1:2, 190
1 Cor. 12:7, 176
1 Cor. 13, 22, 116
1 Cor. 15:14, 25, 125
1 Cor. 15:17, 206
1 Cor. 15:57, 175
1 Cor. 15:6, 8
1 Cor. 16:13-14, 160
1 Jn., 188
1 Jn. 1:8, 113
1 Jn. 3, 132
1 Jn. 3:8, 110
1 Jn. 4:4, 63
1 Jn. 4:8, 200
1 Jn. 5:13, 188
1 Ki. 17, 139
1 Pet. 1:3, 191
1 Pet. 1:6-7, 202
1 Pet. 3:18, 204
1 Pet. 3:18-20, 186
1 Pet. 4:12, 202
1 Sam., 140
1 Thes. 1:12, 196
1 Tim. 1:10, 126
1 Tim. 1:15, 150
1 Tim. 1:17, 182
1 Tim. 2:5, 122
1 Tim. 6:6, 57
2 Chr. 16:9, 137
2 Cor. 4:6, 172
2 Cor. 5:17, 92
2 Cor. 5:18, 70
2 Cor. 5:19-20, 44
2 Cor. 12:9, 46
2 Cor. 5:18-19, 122
2 Pet. 2:4-9, 186
2 Pet. 3:8, 79
2 Pet. 3:9, 80

2 Tim. 4:7, 2
Acts 2:11, 64
Acts 4:12, 204
Acts 4:18, 196
Acts 5:29, 192
Acts 17:26, 70, 120, 208
Col. 1, 86
Col. 2:13, 114
Col. 2:13-14, 62
Col. 3:23, 69
Col. 3:23-24, 173
Col. 3:4, 84
Dan. 7:13-14, 124, 178
Deut. 6:4, 124
Deut. 8:18, 56
Ecc. 3, 103
Eph. 1, 46
Eph. 1:4, 114
Eph. 2:8, 124, 158, 168, 204
Eph. 2:8-10, 55
Eph. 3:19, 90
Eph. 5:32, 66
Eph. 6:10-18, 159
Eph. 6:1-2, 48
Esth. 4:14, 208
Eze. 14:13-14, 186
Gal. 2:20, 64, 84, 184
Gal. 3:20, 164
Gal. 3:28, 164, 204
Gal. 4:6, 124
Gal. 5:1, 156
Gal. 5:11, 154
Gen. 1:1-2, 124
Gen. 1:26-27, 124
Gen. 1:27, 112
Gen. 1:28, 66
Gen. 2:24, 11

Gen. 6, 185
Gen. 6-9, 151
Heb. 2:17, 102
Heb. 4:10, 84
Heb. 4:12, 144
Heb. 4:16, 190
Heb. 11:7, 186
Heb. 12:1, 176
Heb. 12:1-2, 4, 174
Heb. 12:2, 24
Heb. 13:5-6, 58
Heb. 13:8, 182
Hos. 6:6, 187
Isa. 9, 206
Isa. 9:6, 102, 206
Isa. 41:8, 68
Isa. 48:12-16, 124
Isa. 53, 206
Isa. 53:10, 24
Isa. 53:5, 204
Isa. 61:1, 10
Jas. 1:17, 94
Jas. 4:7-8, 190
Job, 68
Joel 2:31, 79
John 1, 177
John 1:10, 98
John 1:14, 97
John 1:2, 206
John 1:3, 56
John 1:5, 105
John 3:16, 88, 114
John 3:18, 62
John 3:3, 191
John 4:10, 50
John 4:26, 50
John 5:17, 142
John 5:24, 62
John 5:30, 63
John 5:7, 50
John 6:35, 50

209

Index